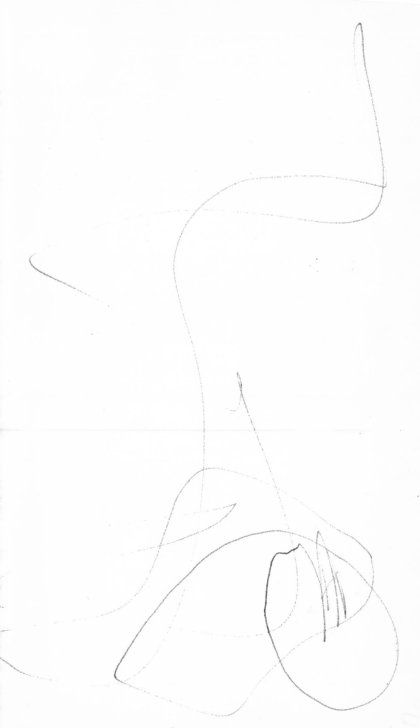

Judaism and the
Christian seminary curriculum

EDITOR

J. Bruce Long

Doctoral candidate
History of Religions, The Divinity School
University of Chicago

EDITORIAL CONSULTANTS

Joseph P. Cahill, S.J.

Associate Professor of Theology
Bellarmine School of Theology
Loyola University

J. Coert Rylaarsdam

Professor of Old Testament
The Divinity School
University of Chicago

Loyola University Press

CHICAGO 60657

ACKNOWLEDGMENTS

Members of the planning committee for the Conference on Judaism and the Christian Seminary Curriculum included the following: Joseph P. Cahill, Joseph DeVault, and William LeSaint, Bellarmine School of Theology, Loyola University; R. W. Mulligan and Paul Mundy, Loyola University; Jerald C. Brauer, Lloyd W. Putnam, Langdon B. Gilkey, J. Coert Rylaarsdam, and Joseph Sittler, The Divinity School, University of Chicago; Monford Harris, College of Jewish Studies, Chicago; Ralph Simon, Congregation Rodfei Zedek, Chicago; Kenneth Newberger, Norman J. Schlossman, Lee Schooler, Chicago Executive Committee, Anti-Defamation League of B'nai B'rith; Hans Adler, ADL Chicago Staff.

A. Abbot Rosen, ADL Midwest Director, was principally responsible for the initiation and direction of the Conference, in which he collaborated with Oscar Cohen, ADL National Program Director.

The Conference was assisted by grants from the Inland Steel-Ryerson Foundation and The Division Fund, which are gratefully acknowledged by the sponsors.

PREFACE

The present volume is the result of a Catholic-Protestant Conference which was convened and sponsored by the Anti-Defamation League of B'nai B'rith. Conference sessions were held in Chicago under the dual auspices of the Bellarmine School of Theology, Loyola University, and The Divinity School, University of Chicago, on March 24 and 25, 1965.

The purposes of the Conference may be stated most conveniently under three headings:

(1) To investigate the strengths and weaknesses of theological curricula in American seminaries--Catholic and Protestant-- with special attention to the question as to whether the training of Christian ministers and theologians contributes in any way to the perpetuation of anti-Semitic attitudes and actions among Christians. By means of papers, comments, and discussions, an attempt was made to evaluate past performance in this area, to discover errors and biases in teaching methods in American seminaries, and to suggest certain improvements in both curricula and methods of instruction as a means of remedying shortcomings.

(2) To enable the representatives of the two Christian communities (and, by extension, the readers of the proposed volume of published proceedings) to see more clearly the character of their respective religious traditions and to determine the religious and social demands of their faiths in the matter of their relations with members of other religious communities, especially the Jewish community.

(3) Consequently, to bring about such changes as would enhance Christian and Jewish relations in America and, conversely, to inhibit any belligerent actions--whether expressed or unexpressed-- between Christians and Jews.

The many purposes and intents which gave birth to and supported this Conference are the outgrowth of an emerging sense that the time is ripe for educational and religious representatives of the major religious communities in America to reevaluate the images and principles by which they define themselves within their own faiths and in their relations with other faiths. With the rapid development of the Ecumenical Movement and of new constructive and affirmative attitudes toward non-Christian religions, it is becoming apparent that many of the ideas and perspectives by which Christians--Catholic and Protestant--have traditionally evaluated their own and other religions require change. New insights have emerged from our experiences in a democratic society where there has occurred a significant renewal of the vitality of many religious groups. Many of those ideas and stances which were once taken for granted as theologically and ethically sound, if not divinely ordained, are now in need of reevaluation and, perhaps, even alteration. The very fact of our living in a pluralistic society, where no single religious group is granted official sanction and where every group is granted the right (officially, at least) to express its own vitality and maintain its own integrity without fear of public censure, has provided every religious group with opportunities for cultural and spiritual enrichment. But this life in the "open society" has, at the same time, generated many dilemmas, not the least crucial of which is how one may exercise his own religious rights without infringing upon the religious rights of others. In light of this novel situation, therefore, new analytic and evaluative perspectives on problems and issues in the area of interreligious relations in America are being called for on many fronts.

A somewhat subtle, but nonetheless crucial, factor at work in this emergent situation is the fact that Jews, individually and collectively, face a unique and untested situation in America today. As the present writer noted in a recent article in Look: "To a certain extent, it has become increasingly easier for a Jew to be a Jew in America since the end of World War II. There is evidence on many fronts that strictures against Jews in various types of employment, in housing, membership in social clubs, and public accommodations are slowly being lifted. The American Jew is experiencing an unprecedented feeling of acceptance, legitimacy and justification. There is a growing sense that a place is being made for him in the structure of the democratic American system." As has been made clear in the final chapter of this volume, the very fact that a conference of this nature was convened by a Jewish organization, the Anti-Defamation League, is indicative of this new emergent spirit of acceptance and legitimacy in American Judaism.

And most noteworthy in recent times is the broadening aspect of the Ecumenical Movement, with roots in the meetings of the World Council of Churches, first in Amsterdam and then in Evanston, which led to the adoption by that international group of a powerful statement concerning the relationship between Judaism and Christianity in the modern world. This statement is quoted in part by Professor Amos N. Wilder in his presentation and, in a sense, reflects the mood of the Conference. We commend to the attention of the readers of this volume a careful reading of the WCC statement in its entirety. This general "liberalizing" tendency in the thinking of Christians about their relations with Jews was given impetus by the adoption of an amended, but nonetheless strong, resolution by the Second Vatican Council, which concluded its final session after the meeting of this Conference.

The resolutions by the WCC and Vatican Council II have stimulated seminarians, both faculty and students, to reflect on the relative merits and demerits of their seminary training and to reconsider in a new light just how that training has affected their relations with Jews in the modern world. It must be stated that a careful examination of the WCC resolutions adopted at both the Amsterdam and New Delhi conferences indicates that the posture of the WCC is ambivalent. The WCC categorically makes a strong condemnation of anti-Semitism; but regarding its attitude toward Judaism, there is still a strong evangelical tone in all its statements. From a Jewish point of view, therefore, much has been left unsaid in the WCC resolutions and statements. It must also be recalled that in spite of the forthrightness of the Vatican Council statement on the Jews, it was revised drastically. As one Catholic delegate to the Council recently stated the matter, the Church Fathers added a series of phrases which changed the document from one of "bold proclamation to one of bold argument." The statements to which he had reference recalled the hostility of Jewish leaders to the Gospels, asserted that Jerusalem missed the hour of her visitation, and reminded Jews that the Church is the new People of God. The exact meaning of the primacy of God's election of the Jews and the nature of the guilt of Christians for much of their past treatment of Jews are issues which neither the Vatican Council document nor the two Protestant statements succeed in resolving; and these issues, therefore, remain on the agenda for further Jewish-Christian conversation.

As already suggested, some of the observations made during this Conference have now become outdated. The Conference was held just after the third session of the Vatican Council had closed, and the speakers refer to many topics and issues which were still in debate before the Council. The book should be read with these facts clearly in mind.

The Conference (and this volume) may be divided into two major parts. The activities of the first day were comprised of the presentations of major papers dealing with the Jewish heritage of Christianity, tangible signs of anti-Semitism in America today, and reviews of the Ecumenical Council from Catholic, Protestant, and Jewish points of view. The second day was given over to a day-long panel discussion dealing with the overall topic of the Conference, namely, "Judaism and the Christian Seminary Curriculum." Five seminarians, representing different divisions of theological education (Old and New Testament Studies, Patristics, Christian Ethics, and Systematic Theology), addressed themselves to the pros and cons of seminary education as it affects interfaith relations. Each presentation was evaluated, and in some cases criticized, by the discussants; and some general suggestions were made as to how alterations could be effectively instituted in the curricula of Catholic and Protestant seminaries.

The Conference was well planned and well attended, with representatives from thirty Christian seminaries. It is fortunate that the proceedings were recorded and can be presented in book form. It is hoped that this volume will make enlightening and provocative reading, not only for specialized seminary professors and students, but also for the general reader who may wish to inform himself on many of the pressing problems which hinder creative interfaith relations in America today.

It is the sincere hope of the planners and participants of the Conference, as well as of the editor of this volume, that the material presented here will clarify the "shape" of Jewish-Christian relations in America and, subsequently, will provoke further discussion of such problems in future Jewish and Christian conferences in seminaries and colleges. If the book can but "create a stir and give a promise," then we will feel that this original pioneering effort in the area of seminary instruction and interfaith relations will have accomplished its main intention.

I cannot conclude this Preface without expressing my great thanks to the two editorial consultants for this volume, Father Joseph P. Cahill and Dr. J. Coert Rylaarsdam, who read and corrected the manuscript before its publication and who made numerous suggestions toward the overall improvement of the book. A special word of thanks must go to Professor Rylaarsdam for his invaluable assistance in the preparation of the Summary and Conclusion.

Chicago, Illinois   J. Bruce Long
March 1, 1966

CONTENTS

ONE

The Jewish heritage of Christianity

William D. Davies
Edward Robinson Professor of Biblical Theology
Union Theological Seminary
Adjunct Professor of Religion, Columbia University

I am honored to have been asked to open this Conference. Into many of the profound theological and metaphysical aspects of the theme of this Colloquium I am not qualified to enter. I presume that I have been honored to open it in virtue of what biblical work I may have done, and it is from the standpoint of a student of the Scriptures that I have proceeded. It will perhaps be universally agreed that the foundation document of the Christian faith is the New Testament; and this, I take it, constitutes the norm for the understanding not only of the Christian Gospel itself but of such questions as the ones which arise from a consideration of the topic I have been asked to discuss: In what ways does Christianity depend upon and profit from its Jewish heritage? I have deemed it prudent, therefore, in the first part of this paper, to present as concisely as possible what the New Testament itself tells us about the interaction of Judaism and Christianity at their earliest encounter.

The definition of terms

To begin, then, let us define our terms. Christianity as a phenomenon in history is so varied, complex and fluid that it is almost impossible to speak of it without distortion and false generalization. In this paper I shall understand Christianity in terms of the New Testament itself. As I noted above, I take the New Testament to be the foundation document of the Christian faith and the source in which we can best recover its genius and ethos. With Christianity as it developed in post-Apostolic times I shall only be concerned in the last section of this paper.

But what do we understand by the Jewish heritage of Christianity? Here we encounter a difficulty. The view has not infrequently been expressed that in the Christian Gospel there is a return from the first century to the great Prophets of Israel. The culmination of the Old Testament is enshrined in the work of the Prophets. After their day, Judaism--a religion of Law, Temple and Syna-gogue--developed in a way wherein the great Prophetic notes were muted: there was a descent from the Prophetic heights. What Jesus of Nazareth did was to appeal to the Prophets, to the submerged Prophetic tradition, against the Judaism of the Law, the Scribe, the Pharisee, the Priest. On this view, by the Jewish heritage of Christianity can only be meant its Old Testament heritage and particularly that of the Prophets. Christianity is a protest against Judaism in favor of the Old Testament. This point of view has been variously expressed. For example, the great R. H. Charles rooted Jesus in Apocalyptic. But what is Apocalyptic? It is the true heir of Old Testament Prophecy which stands over against the legalism of Judaism. It is to this protest against Judaism that Christianity belongs.

As a result of the attitude just indicated, a curious phenomenon arose in the study of the origins of Christianity. It has a parallel in the study of the Classics. I recall that when I took an Honor's degree in Classical Greek, the authors I had to study reached down as far as Aristotle. After this there was a jump to Latin literature. The whole literature of the Hellenistic Age, including the slightly barbaric New Testament, was ignored. It was not until some years after I had taken my degree, when I heard the Classical scholar R. H. Charlesworth, that I came to realize

2

that the Hellenistic Age is, in a sense, the flowering of the Classical Age and that the latter cannot be rightly understood without the former. The tacit assumption of my Greek teachers had been that Classical literature stopped around the time of Aristotle.

So was it in much Christian treatment of Christian origins. Since Jesus was thought to be rooted in the Prophets, what came after the Prophets was largely ignored. The whole complex development of Judaism in the post-Exilic period tended to be treated very scantily by New Testament scholars, just as the Hellenistic Age was neglected by Classical scholars. When scholars referred to the Jewish heritage of Christianity, they meant primarily the Prophetic heritage and secondarily the Apocalyptic heritage. The Pharisaic, Scribal or Rabbinic tradition was regarded as that which Christianity rejected.

This almost traditional approach to the Jewish heritage of Christianity we must abandon. I shall assume that not only the Prophetic tradition but the whole complex of Judaism is meant by the phrase "the Jewish heritage." That is, Judaism as well as the Old Testament constitutes the heritage of Christianity. There are three main reasons for insisting on this.

First, the old distinction drawn between priestly, legalistic Judaism and Prophetic Judaism has broken down.

Secondly, there has been a rejection of any sharp distinction between Apocalyptic and Pharisaism.

Thirdly, a deeper Jewish and Christian understanding of the first century, often informed by the agony of our time, has made it easier for us to do justice to the legal tradition in Judaism.

By the Jewish heritage of Christianity, therefore, I refer to the totality of Judaism as the inheritance of Christianity.

The relationship of Christianity
and Judaism in the light
of the New Testament

Having thus defined our terms, let us now ask what the relationship is between Christianity and Judaism, first of all, in the light of the New Testament itself. The New Testament presents this relationship in at least three ways. Let us look at each in turn.

First, there are documents in which there is little awareness of any essential break between Judaism and Christianity. Jesus has come as the Messiah, but the essential structure of Judaism has remained virtually unaltered. Acceptance of Jesus does not mean any radical break with Jewish practice or belief. All that has happened in Christianity is that Judaism is now in possession of its long-awaited Messiah; but his advent has demanded very little change. The earliest Christians, the Judaizers and other Jewish Christians, who held this position have left few traces in the New Testament itself, although their presence can easily be discerned moving shadowily behind the pages of the New Testament, especially in the Pauline Epistles. But they have left us noncanonical materials which are fairly substantial in extent. The Christianity which these reveal has been examined anew and given great prominence by Professor H. J. Schoeps of Erlangen. He finds Jewish Christianity to have been the chief bulwark in the primitive Church against Marcion and the threat of Gnosticism. That this Christianity disappeared, leaving very little trace, is no indication of its real significance in history. From the point of view of Jewish Christianity, the Christian faith is a reformation or revision of Judaism involving little radical newness. It is, indeed, merely Judaism with an addendum--Jesus the Messiah. We may agree with Schoeps that the disappearance of Jewish Christianity may be no indication of its significance at the time when it flourished, but many have regarded that disappearance as almost inevitable because it provided no ultimate raison d'être for Christianity alongside Judaism.

At the opposite extreme, we find, in certain documents of the New Testament, the claim that the relation of Christianity to Judaism is one of sharp antithesis. This comes to clearest expression in the Fourth Gospel, where there is a sustained interpretation of the Christian faith which emphasizes that it has replaced Judaism. On this view, Christianity is a revolution which so transforms Judaism that the latter can be regarded as superseded. It is true that the Fourth Gospel urges that salvation is from the Jews and uses categories that are derived from Judaism to expound Jesus's significance, but it does look away from Judaism also. The newness of the Gospel is such that the old order of the waterpots has given place to the new wine of the Gospel. The quintessence of John's attitude may perhaps be understood in the story of Mary and the beloved disciple at the cross: But meanwhile near the cross where Jesus hung stood his mother, with her sister, Mary wife of Clopas, and Mary of Magdala. Jesus saw his mother, with the disciple whom he loved standing beside her. He said to her, "Mother, there is your son"; to the disciple, "There is your mother." And from that moment the disciple took her into his home. Mary is the mother of Jesus. She is now handed over to the respectful care of his disciple. Her function is over. If Mary here stands for Judaism, the implication is clear: Judaism is the aged mother; she is honored and cherished, but a new order to which she has given birth replaces her. She is the relation between Judaism and Christianity.

So far we have noted two attitudes toward Judaism on the part of New Testament Christians. For some, the Gospel is a revision, though not a radical one, of Judaism; for others, the Gospel supersedes Judaism as its antithesis. We now come to the third attitude. It is best represented perhaps in Matthew and in Hebrews. The attitude may be expressed in terms of Matthew 5:17: "I came not to destroy but to complete." The immediate context in Matthew concerns the Law, but the attitude can be extended to cover the whole of Judaism. The Christian Gospel has brought to full fruition the intent of Judaism. It has not only fulfilled the Jewish hope for a Messiah; it has brought with it a new temple, a new law, a new sacrifice, a new people. In all these cases the adjective "new" is not meant to indicate antithesis, but fulfillment. What in Judaism was shadowy, tentative and preparatory is now fully realized in Christ. Readers of the Epistle to the Hebrews do not need to be reminded of the way in which the theology of that Epistle is built upon the theology of Judaism as its "completion."

There is one figure, possibly the major figure of the New Testament (apart, of course, from Jesus), whom it is difficult to place in any of the categories already indicated. Paul has been regarded, particularly by Jewish scholars but also by Protestants dominated by Luther, as having broken with Judaism in a radical fashion. Jewish scholars have accused Paul of breaking down the fence of the Torah, and Christian scholars have set his doctrine of "justification by faith" over against the emphasis in Judaism on "salvation by works." But there can be little question that Paul remained throughout his life, in his own mind, within the pale of Judaism. Christ was for him the end (Τέλος) of Judaism, not in the sense of its annulment, but of its fulfillment. By and large, I should classify Paul with Hebrews and Matthew rather than with the Fourth Gospel. To him, also, Christianity is not the antithesis of Judaism but its culmination.

The New Testament, therefore, presents us with three main alternatives. How are we to evaluate these? We can do so only in the light of recent scholarship on Christian origins. We turn, then, to the second part of this paper.

The relationship of
Christianity and Judaism
in the light of recent scholarship

The alternatives to which we have referred can only be evaluated in the light of what we know of Judaism in the first century. Fortunately, since the end of the last century, there has emerged a new understanding and appreciation of first-century Judaism. This has a twofold source.

First, in Christian scholarship the impulse for the study of first-century Judaism came from the work of Johannes Weiss, who insisted on the eschatological or apocalyptic nature of the message of Jesus. The liberal approach to the historical Jesus was faced with the challenge of the eschatological Christ. The result of the challenge was to drive liberal Christian scholars to examine the nature of first-century Judaism. It is from the end of the last century that Christian concentration on first-century Judaism dates. There followed, in the twentieth century, a stream of works dealing with that period--to our vast enrichment. I name especially the works of Dalman, Schurer, Bousset, Moore, Bonsirven and Herford.

But, secondly, alongside the work of Christian scholars, there also appeared many works by Jewish scholars. In England especially there was a rich cooperation between Jewish and Christian scholars, usually centering in New Testament Seminars. From these emerged the works of Abrahams, Loewe and David Daube, while the names of Schechter and Montefiore will also be familiar.

As a result of the work of these scholars, and many others, there has emerged a far more realistic and sympathetic understanding of first-century Judaism. This is, I venture to think, particularly the case in British and American scholarship, where there has generally been a great readiness to deal justly by Judaism.

What are the results of this new assessment of first-century Judaism? Roughly we may see a parallel in recent scholarship to those three attitudes which we discovered in the New Testament.

First, in the initial flush of enthusiasm with the discovery of the richness and profundity of first-century Judaism, there were some scholars who so emphasized these that they failed to recognize any fundamental differences between it and Christianity. Reading the works of some of these scholars on first-century Judaism is like reading a long panegyric. This is to some extent true of R. Travers Herford, the pioneer Englishman who set the sympathetic stream in motion. No one can deny the magnitude of his contribution, but few can deny also that his treatment of first-century Judaism tends to be sentimentalized--as sentimentalized, let us say, as that of Claude Montefiore. My old neighbor Dr. James Parkes (≪ quem honoris causa nomino ≫) may also be claimed perhaps to have been so anxious to do justice to Judaism that at times he falls into a myopic understanding of the Christian faith. He finds, for example, the faith centered in Sinai to be a communal faith, over against which he sets the faith centered in Calvary which is an individual faith. Dr. Parkes' sympathy with Judaism may seem to have led him to neglect aspects of Chris-tianity which are even central to Christianity, though he himself would deny this. The same flush of enthusiasm, I believe, governs my eminent predecessor, Dr. F. C. Grant, in his well-known work ≪ The New Testament and Ancient Judaism ≫. And may I be allowed to recall that my own work has been described, wrongly I venture to think, as pro-Semitic. The swing of the pendulum in British and American scholarship has seemed, at times, radical. But it is wise to recognize that violent reactions are seldom acceptable in the long run. The cause of Jewish-Christian mutual respect must be founded on a sober recognition and assessment of facts, not on enthusiasms.

Secondly, there are scholars who have been little touched in their interpretation of New Testament Christianity by the new empathy with Judaism which has emerged. I shall name only Pro-fessor Bultmann. His treatment of Judaism in his well-known book ≪ Jesus and the Word ≫ is a moving and illuminating one, but he uses it as a background against which Jesus is to be understood; and in his later theology, Bultmann's understanding of the Judaic roots of Christianity does not emerge as a positive one.

Thirdly, however, over a broad section of New Testament scholarship there has increasingly emerged the recognition that the Christian faith is not only rooted in Judaism but is its ful-fillment, and that Christianity carries over into its own life the structure of Judaism. The emergence of this awareness has been attractively set forth in an article by Professor Markus Barth in the first volume of the ≪ Ecumenical Review ≫ under the title "The Challenge of St. Paul" (Vol. 1, No. 1, pp. 58-81). This article will be familiar to most of those gathered here, and its details need not be repeated. In short, when all exaggerations have been reckoned with, it is increasingly evident that the relationship between Judaism and Christianity is far more positive and complementary than the mists of history and religious nar-rowness had allowed us to see. Here, during this Colloquium, we can only hope to indicate the main outlines of the case. For the sake of convenience, we shall ask how the dependence of Christianity on Judaism emerges in three areas: the theological, the ethical and the organizational.

Let us begin with the theological dependence of the Christian faith on Judaism. We shall assume that the Christian faith is concerned from first to last with the reality and purpose of the Living God who governs and sustains the universe. This monotheism it shares with and derives from Judaism. The world into which early Christianity emerged was one familiar with gods many and lords many; it was only able to assume monotheism because it had been born within Judaism. But the achievement of monotheism had not been easy within Judaism. It was only after the fires of the Exile that it can be said that monotheism became the faith of most religious Jews. Down to the last of the canonical Prophets the reality of other gods was by no means generally rejected. In the strictest sense, monotheism was a costly achievement within Judaism; and Christianity entered into the riches of Judaism at this point. There is never a suggestion in the New Testament that the God whom Christians presuppose is not the very same God worshipped in Judaism. The God who speaks to Christians in Jesus Christ is the God of Abraham, Isaac and Jacob. The God who wrought redemption in Christ is also the God who brought the Jews out of the land of Egypt, led them through the wilderness, spoke to them at Sinai, gave them the Prophets, brought them safely out of Babylon. Christianity has never doubted that it is the God who spoke to Israel in diverse ways and manners who also speaks in his Son.

It is true that there have arisen in the Church those who have tried to deny this. In the second century there were the Marcionites; and in the twentieth, those who have tried to oust the Hebrew Bible from the services of the Church as an outmoded volume which can only be read seriously as good literature, touched perhaps with good morality. But such people have failed to move Christians from the conviction that the God of the Old Covenant is also the God of the New Covenant, that the voice heard at Sinai and at Calvary is the voice of the same God.

As a result, the Old Testament is still part of the Christian canon of Scripture, and has thus become, we hope, bone of our bone. Through it, Christians, to some extent at least, breathe the same air as Jewry. As a recent Pope has expressed it, "Spiritually we are all Semites." This identity of origin then-- the fact that both Judaism and Christianity purport to have their

8

origin in a revelation of the same God, the One God--naturally gives them a peculiar intimacy. We may confidently claim that Christianity owes its belief in the One God to Judaism.

But, apart from this basic fact, we can go further. The early Church not only assumed the God of Judaism; it also assumed the sacredness of the Scriptures of Judaism--that is, it took over from Judaism a body of tradition, the Old Testament. True, Judaism had not finally fixed its canon when Jesus appeared, but it did already have a written Torah--including Law, Prophets and Writings--which it accepted as authoritative. This body of tradition, in written form, the Church took over. The significance of this fact cannot be exaggerated. Because the Church, in taking over the Scriptures, did so in the conviction that its own faith was rooted in and was the fulfillment of the Old Testament. This is another way of saying that the Church understood itself in the light of the Old Testament. Among the myriad consequences which flow from this basic fact, two in particular may be emphasized.

First, like its acceptance of the God of Abraham and Isaac and Jacob, the acceptance of the Old Testament tied Christianity forever to the stream of tradition which we know as Judaism. As did Judaism itself, so also the Church understood itself in the light of a particular history. It placed itself in the same stream of revelation as did Judaism; it tied itself not only to the God of Abraham and Isaac and Jacob but to the concrete history of his dealings with Israel, to Moses, Elijah, the Prophets, the sweet singers and the priests of Israel. The history of Judaism became part of the history of the Church. This means that Christianity made Judaism an inseparable part of its own history. Christianity is in a particular stream of history; it can never be detached from this without ceasing to be itself.

But, secondly, in taking the Old Testament as its Sacred Scripture, the early Church did more than recognize its historical connection and even continuity with Judaism; it provided itself with the concepts, terminology and motifs through which it was both to understand itself and interpret its faith to the world. In short, Judaism provided what Professor C. H. Dodd has taught us to call the "substructure of Christian theology." New Testament Christianity, even in its Johannine form, is articulated in the language of Judaism.

This is made most clear in an area which has attracted much attention in the scholarship of the last few decades, namely, the use of quotations from the Old Testament in the New. These quotations are not merely strange bits of jigsaw puzzles wrested from the Old Testament, but indications of the way in which the very structure of Jewish thought determines that of Christian thought. The evidence for such a statement is so copious that no attempt to present it can be made here. I shall merely illustrate how Jewish thinking is the form of Christian thinking by a few examples of first a more general and then a more particular kind.

First, let us look at the broad way in which the early Christians thought of the Christian era or dispensation. There are two figures or metaphors which are familiar in the New Testament. The first is that of a new Creation, along with which there go certain con-comitants such as the concept of Jesus the Messiah as the second Adam. In these broad categories did the early Christians under-stand themselves, and these categories were derived from Judaism. (At this point, the members of the Colloquium are referred to my book « Paul and Rabbinic Judaism », pp. 36 ff., for detailed sup-port of the claim made. It is not possible to reproduce the material fully in such a paper as this. The same applies to my treatment of the New Exodus. I ask the members' indulgence.) Another broad category derived from Judaism is that of the New Exodus, with its concomitant of Jesus as the New Moses. The thought that there is a real parallel between the events of the Exodus and those which inaugurated the Christian era is frequent in the New Testament. The evidence for this in the Gospel of Matthew, and to some extent in Mark, I have presented recently in a volume entitled « The Setting of the Sermon on the Mount ». It reemerges clearly in Paul and, by way of antithesis, in the Fourth Gospel and else-where. There is no need to labor the obvious. The early Church understood itself as having undergone a new Exodus; it derived this basic category for its self-understanding from Judaism. Other major categories which it also employed are derived from the same source--for example, the Kingdom of God, in the Syn-optics, and Eternal Life, in the Fourth Gospel, to mention only the most obvious.

But, in the second place, it is important to recognize that in the minutiae of its theological activity, through and in which it reflected upon its own existence, the early Church thought es-sentially in the categories of Judaism. Here again, it is impos-sible to set forth the evidence in this paper. In my work on « Paul and Rabbinic Judaism » I sought to show how the main motifs in Paulinism--the Flesh, the Last Adam, the Old and the New Man, Christ as the Wisdom of God, Obedience, Resurrection --are all best understood against the background of Pharisaic Judaism. In other documents of the New Testament, including

10

those which have most often been connected with the Hellenistic world, the same could be shown to be true. In this paper I shall only draw upon two examples, both from Paul, where it seems to me that the thought of the Apostle cannot adequately be understood apart from either the Old Testament or Judaism. The examples are chosen because the matter with which they deal has frequently been taken to point to Hellenistic sources. The two examples are the concept of being "in Christ" and that of the "Body of Christ." (Again, for details, I refer to ≪ Paul and Rabbinic Judaism≫, pp. 87 ff. et passim and pp. 53 ff.)

Even if the two particular examples which I have here chosen to illustrate the dependence of the early Church on Paul be rejected, there are others which could be used to attest to the same point. Few would not now agree that primitive Christianity, both in its grand outlines or major categories and in its details, is dependent upon Judaism. In this sense, the very matrix of Christianity is Judaism; the former is of the very bone of the latter.

Professor Jean Daniélou, in his significant work ≪ Théologie du Judéo-Christianisme≫, has sought to show--with much success--that its Semitic substructure continued to inform Christian theology right down to Nicaea. The first sentences in his volume read: "La théologie chrétienne utilisera à partir des Apologistes les instruments intellectuels de la philosophie grecque. Mais auparavant il y a en une première théologie de structure semitique." We might go even further than Daniélou (who confines his attention chiefly to Apocalyptic Judaism) in insisting that after Nicaea also, simply because of the perpetuation of the New Testament and Old Testament in the life of the Church (not to speak here of other currents) as its foundation documents, this Semitic substructure continued to exert its influence. Unfortunately, the full extent of this influence has never been recognized because of Christian ignorance of Judaism. There is little doubt that a deeper understanding of the governing concepts of first-century Judaism than has hitherto even been aimed at would throw a flood of light on early Christianity. This has come home with particular force to me in extended discussions with Professor Abraham Heschel. Phenomena such as the Resurrection, the Ascension, and indeed the whole range of early Christian concern, can only be illumined for us by a deeper penetration of Pharisaic Judaism.

As in the realm of theology, so in the realm of ethics the debt of Christianity to Judaism is profound, but its precise nature is difficult to assess. In a broad sense, Judaism and Christianity have an identity of moral concern over a wide area. Just as the aim of Christianity is to give its adherents what the New Testament calls "eternal life," both in this world and in the age to come, so too the Torah has been given to Israel that men might live by its precepts. Life in conformity to the will of God is the aim of both Judaism and Christianity. Both Church and Synagogue pray that the rule or kingdom of God may come and his will be done, so that the Lord may be one and his people one.

And we may claim that the ethical tradition of Judaism has passed over into Christianity. Jesus was, in a certain sense, a rabbi no less than a prophet. Both the method and very largely the substance and form of his ethical teaching were rabbinical. Nourished in the Synagogue, Jesus gave his followers much of the ethic of the Synagogue. The moral demands of Jesus as set forth in the Sermon on the Mount are introduced by the words: "Do not suppose that I have come to abolish the Law and the prophets; I did not come to abolish, but to complete." (Matthew 5:17.) The teaching of Jesus is presented as the culmination-- the full flowering--of the moral tradition of Judaism. This concept must be given its full weight. So also, the motivation for the good life in Christianity and Judaism must be recognized as similar. For both, gratitude to God is the dynamic of the good life; and obedience to the will of God, its content. It is thus possible to speak of a Judeo-Christian ethical tradition which Jews and Christians have in common.

I am not unaware of the difficulty which emerges at this point. It is brought to sharp focus in St. Paul. Is it not true that Paul rejected the very essence of Judaism--salvation by the mitzvah-- in favor of salvation by faith and the spirit? Is it not also true that the New Testament generally forsakes at least the oral tradition of Judaism and concentrates on the strictly moral tradition of the Old Testament? Does it not so elevate the command of agape that it depresses vast stretches of the ethical tradition of Judaism and ignores it? On this, one can only assert that, however far primitive Christianity departed from the form which moral concern assumed in Judaism, the reality of that concern remained. That the Gospel is nowhere set forth without a moral demand we owe to Judaism. I should go further. Christianity took over from Judaism a fundamentally covenantal structure. Within this covenantal structure, morality is fundamental. Nowhere in the New Testament, because of its rootage in Judaism, does the moral demand cease to be endemic to Christianity. This is as true of Paul as of Matthew. However much it may be claimed that Christianity jettisoned the moral-legal tradition of Judaism, it retained the heart of the matter. The New Commandment of John, the Golden Rule of Matthew, the Law of the Messiah of Paul, the New Covenant of Hebrews--they all presuppose that the "commandment" remains inseparable from the Gospel. This is part of Christianity's abiding debt to Judaism. It may be admitted that the form of morality in Christianity has come to differ from that of Judaism, but the concern with morality as the Divine Imperative has remained in the daughter faith.

Turning now to organizational aspects, we find here another area where the Christian faith is indebted to Judaism, for Judaism and Christianity reveal an identity of conception as to the means whereby the purpose of God is to be achieved. In Judaism the community of God's people, the Israel of God, is the agent of God in the world. It was a people that God chose at the Exodus to be his messengers in the world, and in a real sense the Old Testament is the record of God's attempts to prepare for himself a peculiar people that should make known his ways. But what is true of Judaism is also true of New Testament Christianity: God's purposes are to be achieved through a community--the New Israel of God, the Church. In the New Testament the Church is, in fact, Israel in a new manifestation of its history. This is so clear that, even in writing to mixed and befuddled Corinthian converts, Paul can speak of the Jews of the Exodus as the "fathers" of Christians without having to explain what he meant. That God's purpose is to be fulfilled, not only and not chiefly by isolated individuals but by the life of a witnessing community, is as true of Christianity as of Judaism. And the relation of the New Israel to the Old is not simply one of antithesis but of fulfillment and continuity. The communal self-awareness of Christianity stems from Judaism.

Moreover, it is not only in the concept of the Church as constituting the true Israel that the New Israel is indebted to the Old. The very forms which the New Testament uses to express the new life "in Christ" it borrows from Judaism. In the early years of this century, under the influence of the school of Comparative Religion, the two sacraments of Baptism and the Lord's Supper were traced to Hellenistic religions, the Mysteries. But more recent work has at least opened the possibility that these two central moments of the Christian community are to be understood in terms of baptismal and Passover practices within Judaism.

When we turn to disciplinary practice, spasmodically revealed in the New Testament, we find dependence on disciplinary forms already evolved in Judaism. This is true for example of the "manual of discipline" which emerges in Matthew 18, where both Rabbinic and Qumran usages seem to be taken over by the Matthaean Church for its own purposes. A Jewish origin is suggested also by Paul's disciplinary activity.

In forms of worship and in ministerial structure, the influence of the Synagogue again emerges in the organizational aspects of the life of the Church. Both the forms of Christian worship and the structure of the various ministries in the Church can be shown to have been influenced by the Synagogue at various points, but to illustrate these two factors in detail would prolong this paper inordinately, so the reader must be content with a mere reference to a vast area of concern.

We may now briefly sum up wherein lies the debt of Christianity to Judaism. To the latter the former owes the awareness of the Living God, who is no absentee landlord but is actively engaged in the history of those whom he created. The sense of history as the sphere of Divine Activity, and not as the blind, meaningless outcome of a fortuitous conglomeration of atoms or the ever-recurring expression of uncontrolled and uncontrollable cosmic force, of fate and death--this Christianity owes to Judaism. That is, it owes to Judaism the recognition of the meaningfulness of the stage on which the human drama is played. To this same source the Church owes its awareness of the demand which is laid upon it--its moral seriousness and its self-awareness as a community.

The relationship of Christianity
and Judaism in the light of history:
How Christianity benefits from this

We are now faced with the second half of the question put to me by the Colloquim: How does its rootage in Judaism profit Christianity? That is, at first encounter, a very ungracious question. It is as if a daughter asked how she profits from her mother. The daughter who asks such a question immediately becomes suspect as an ungrateful jade. For Christians to ask how they profit from Judaism is to reveal a crass insensitivity to the rock whence they were hewn. It will be recognized, therefore, that I shall deal with this part of my question, expressed in this form, under protest. To change the metaphor, for Christianity to question the value of its dependence upon Judaism is for a dog to bite the hand that fed him.

Not only so, but this second part of the question raises all sorts of comparative questions with which I am hardly competent to deal.

In the course of its history, Christianity has undergone Hellenization, Romanization and Westernization. In our day it is likely
to undergo Asianization and Americanization. The second half
of our question demands a comparative estimate of the value for
Christianity of the various influences which it has absorbed and
which have informed it. The problem already emerges in the
New Testament itself, where Hellenistic and Roman factors are
already at work--even in Paul himself. In emphasizing the importance of its Jewish root for Christianity in the following para-
graphs, I shall not attempt to evaluate it in comparison with other
factors. Let me only say at the outset that I cannot accept the
view that a rigid adherence to its Jewish root alone would have
sufficed for Christianity. Nor can I imagine that the elimination
of Roman and Greek and Western influences on, and from formulations of, Christianity would be salutary. Christianity, no less
than Judaism, cannot refuse to meet the challenge of new cultures
and to some extent absorb their structures and thought-forms.
And a return to the "simplest" Semitic expression of Christianity,
in its neatness, would be as futile as it would be impossible. For
example, there are those who would confine the meaning and
significance of the Gospel to the eschatological categories of
primitive Christianity, who would retain the Semitic understanding
of history as an essential of the Gospel while rejecting every
Hellenization of the faith and every attempt to give another con-
ceptual form to it. But the rejection of Hellenism in the understanding of Christianity is not a real possibility for us. Historically,
even Judaism itself was partially Hellenzied before the advent of
Christianity; and the New Testament itself, Semitic in substructure
as it is, is nevertheless Hellenistic in its dress. Moreover, I cannot concede that Christianity itself demands a resistance to all
non-Semitic modes of interpreting our Christian experience.

But having said this, let me hasten to add that, historically,
Christianity has often been more prone to accommodate itself to
new worlds than to remain true to its Semitic rootage. The question set to me--"How does Christianity profit from its Jewish
heritage?"--might perhaps be more aptly phrased: "How could
Christianity have profited from its Jewish heritage?" Because,
in fact, the history of Christendom, by revealing its neglect of
Judaism, makes clear how it could have profited from it. I can
best answer the question by pointing out how, historically,
Christianity has suffered from its neglect of Judaism. Our approach, then, will be an indirect one. We shall cast a quick
glance over the history of Christianity, pointing out how the

neglect of its rootedness in Judaism has impoverished the Church. In this negative way, we can be led to an appreciation of some of the positive values of the connection between Christianity and Judaism.

In view of the intimacy between the two religions to which we have referred above, it is not surprising that in the first century there continued a living dialogue between many Jews and Christians. Leading rabbis were often in close contact with Christians. But as time went on, the two movements became separated. The recognition of a common heritage was submerged by concentration on the points of difference.

The central point of difference has always been the evaluation of Jesus of Nazareth as the Messiah. But there were others: the evaluation and place of the Law, the significance of the Church as the New Israel. Is the Law superseded in the coming of Christ? Has the Old Israel any longer a raison d'être now that the New Israel has come? What difference would it make if synagogues and their endless reading of the Law ceased to exist? These and other points of contention gradually became the points of concentration.

Further changes came as the Church spread more and more into the Latin world of the West, the Hellenistic world and the Slavonic world, and as it became the established church of both the Western and Eastern empires. With the growth of its social and political prestige, the religious emphases the Church had shared with Judaism became increasingly muted. In new climates of thought, what had once been in essence a Semitic religion became Hellenized. Gradually, as the minority Christian community became the dominant one and Judaism found itself subservient to its own daughter faith, the dialogue became a war-- a shameful war.

The price paid by Judaism has been unrelenting suffering. But the price paid by Christianity has been no less real, though less obvious. It has paid the price of shame and guilt for its bloody past. Its own life has been emaciated by the neglect of its own roots. It would be impossible to deal adequately here with the price paid by the Church for its neglect of, and abuse of and contempt for its own mother, the Synagogue. But certain lines of thought may be suggested.

It might first be argued that the Church ran the risk of forgetting what I may call the "democratic" note in Judaism. The emergence of what seems, to many outsiders at least, an almost "militarily" hierarchical organization in the West and of a hierarchical system dominated by the State in the East is connected with the Church's failure to understand itself as the "people of God," as had the Old Israel. By sitting loose to the more humble Synagogue, the organism Church more easily developed into an organization, a community stratified like the surrounding society and organized in terms of a ministry separated from, though maintained by, a subservient laity.

The "imperialization" of the Church in the East and West was possible only because it refused to be true to the democratic genius of the Synagogue. A Jew in the Middle Ages expressed this point dramatically: "Through the establishment of the episcopate of the Church in Rome, the Christians may be considered Romans." (Cited by H. J. Schoeps, ≪ The Jewish-Christian Argument ≫.) The Church preferred to imitate imperial forms rather than follow the more modest forms of the Synagogue. The results we know--in the Papal pretensions of the Middle Ages, in the ridiculous clerical pomposities that still lay so much religious activity open to the charge of empty vanity.

It is significant that the changes being urged at Vatican II in favor of collegiality and decentralization have found their inspiration in the rediscovery of the biblical understanding of the Church as the "people of God"--an understanding which could not help but produce a revolt against any rigidly hierarchical organization. The Reformation moved in the direction of simplicity in religion, and away from Papal regimentation, precisely because it deliberately returned to the biblical roots of the faith.

Few would deny that the true democratization of religion still has a long way to go. One way in which its progress can be helped is by the resumption of Christian dialogue with the Synagogue, from which democracy, in the sense in which I here use the word, has never departed.

Associated with the democratic tradition of the Synagogue is its moral tradition. I am fully aware that the Church has not been without its strong moral concerns. I am also aware that the Synagogue has often produced a most banal and barren moralism. But there can be little doubt that when the Synagogue and the Church parted company, the Church was morally impoverished. The moral tradition of Judaism, rooted in the Old Testament and interpreted by Scribe and Rabbi, gave to the Synagogue a depth of moral sensitivity and a communal awareness that were impressive. As the Church became more and more Hellenized and Romanized and Erastian, in large measure it lost these. Two developments in particular may be connected with the decline of the Church's living contact with the Synagogue.

First, the separation of the religious life from the common life of man grew apace. The most glaring example is the monastic movement, wherein the forces of moral seriousness were channeled to the cloister and the nunnery. A double morality arose: a higher morality for life out of the world, a lower one for life in the world. The affirmation of all life as sacred, which has always characterized the Synagogue, was ignored; and the Christian world became divided into clerical and lay people, secular and sacred institutions, holy persons and holy things set over against unholy persons and unholy things. Nor did Protestantism escape the continuance of this sacred-secular dualism. The wholeness of life that Judaism has always stressed was lost. The divorce of religion from life is part of the price paid for our neglect of the Synagogue. (The concept of the wholeness of life remained in Judaism despite the separation of things clean and unclean, despite the separation from the world involved in keeping the Law. Throughout all this "separation," Judaism was attempting to take seriously the application of the Law--i.e., God's will--to all life.)

Secondly, and not unrelated to this, is the loss--more especially in Protestantism this time--of the communal awareness that the Synagogue has always fostered. Catholicism has always preserved a certain communal awareness, but within Protestantism, despite its biblicism, a rabid individualism in piety and life has often reared its head. The strong communal sense of the Synagogue, within which each suffered for the other in the interest of the whole, was often lost, and the most blatant forms of individualism (often another name for callousness) found the benediction of religion. Reinhold Niebuhr has often said that what impressed him most in his fight for social justice was that most of those who were fighting beside him were Jews and Roman Catholics. His experience is not unique.

There can be little question that the divorce of the Church from the Synagogue was accompanied by a lessening of its social awareness. This separation meant a great loss within the Church: it resulted in a dilution of that rugged, democratic, moral, prophetic tradition out of which the Gospel arose. But Christendom could not long deny its own origins without paying the price even more directly from outside. The Semitic thrust behind Christendom which was suppressed across the centuries reasserted itself in the last century. And it did so in a strange quarter.

Within a Christendom in which the faith had increasingly lost its Judaic flavor, there arose a mighty secular protest, that of

18

international Marxism. Marx himself had little truck with Judaism, which he regarded with contempt. Nevertheless, that he was a Jew is symbolic--symbolic of the fact that a Christendom that denies its Judaic root does so at its peril. Marxism is largely the protest of the secular world against a Christianity that has sold its birth-right and become so conformed to this world that it has failed to register its protest against the exploitation of men. Marxism is the nemesis of a "de-Judaized" Christianity.

In this sense, there is a connection between Moscow and what is going on now in Rome. It is no accident that as the vitality of Communism is recognized, the Church should turn to its links with the Synagogue, the neglect of which has led to this massive protest against the false spirituality of so much of Christendom.

The above broad--and, I fear, too bold--review of Christian history reveals how the Church could have profited from the Synagogue, but failed. Where the Jewish rootage of Christianity is neglected, the Church tends to lose awareness of the Living God at work in history in favor of otherworldliness, mysticism and gnosis; it tends to lessen the astringent moral imperative of the call to live out its faith in the world; it tends to lose aware-ness of itself as above all a people, and not a structured organ-ization, and to forsake the world for the wrong reasons. Where the benefits of Judaism are consciously cherished, these aber-rations can be avoided. But it is only now, beyond the great and terrible divide of Hitler and beyond the great and glorious divide of John XXIII, that we are at last speaking about these things openly. At long last we can confess our contrition before the slaughter of Jews in Christian Europe; we can repent for the neglect of the Church's Jewish heritage. We are given in Roman-ism and Protestantism a unique opportunity to open the gates of the Church to the Synagogue--that is, to renew the dialogue that history has broken. The conditions are present for Church and Synagogue to coexist in mutual stimulus, respect and fruition. That the benefits to the Church would be enormous we have no doubt; that the Synagogue would also benefit we cannot but hope. When Paul thought of what Israel could give to the Church, he could only use the amazing expression "life from the dead." There can be few more urgent tasks for the Church than to prepare for this dialogue, that it might really be a dialogue and not a solil-oquy, that it might be marked by the radical frankness which alone makes genuine dialogue possible.

TWO

Christian beliefs and anti-Semitism:
report on the California study

Charles Y. Glock
Director, Survey Research Center
University of California, Berkeley

Under a grant from the Anti-Defamation League of B'nai B'rith, the Survey Research Center of the University of California is currently engaged in a five-year research program to assess the extent and to determine the causes of anti-Semitism in contemporary America. This program, stimulated by the widespread and overt incidents of anti-Semitism which swept America in the winter and spring of 1959-60, is involving us in a series of studies, each looking into a different facet of the phenomenon of anti-Semitism. In the end, the results of these studies will be published in seven volumes by Harper and Row.

One of the studies in which we are engaged is investigating the role of Christian beliefs in contemporary anti-Semitism, and it is to a brief summary of the results of this study that I will address my remarks this afternoon. Our study, while still not quite complete, is nevertheless far enough along so that the main tenor of our findings is now firmly established.

The idea that Christianity and anti-Semitism are historically linked is not likely to generate much debate. The evidence is widespread and firm that much of the anti-Semitism of the past was stimulated and sustained by Christian fervor and zeal. Our present inquiry is directed essentially to finding out whether or not the link has been broken. Is there still a strong religious element in current anti-Semitism? Or, as some observers have suggested, are Christianity and the Church more appropriately characterized now as important vehicles through which individuals are led to transcend latent feelings of prejudice?

The theory which informed our inquiry conceived that any remnant of a connection between Christian beliefs and anti-Semitism would be the result of a persistence among Christians to hold to a rigidly orthodox faith and to do so in what we have called "particularistic" terms. By orthodox faith, we mean a literal interpretation of traditional Christian dogma as exemplified in unequivocal belief in the divinity of Christ, in the virgin birth, in biblical miracles, in the devil, and the like. By particularism, we mean a disposition to see Christian truth as the only religious truth; to conceive, for example, of a belief in Christ as the only path to salvation.

Our theory did not suggest that orthodox belief, in and of itself, is sufficient to generate anti-Semitism. Neither did we suggest that anti-Semitism of a secular kind follows directly from orthodoxy when it is combined with particularism. The process, as we envisaged it, is more complex than this, and should it occur, we conceived it to proceed as follows.

To begin with, we made no assumptions about how many American Christians hold to a firmly orthodox faith. This was a question to be decided empirically. We did postulate at the outset, however, that orthodox Christians would be highly predisposed to be particularistic ones also. Orthodoxy and particularism need not necessarily go together. One can easily imagine an orthodox Hindu who would acknowledge the equal validity of Christian faith. For reasons endemic to Christian history, however, it is more difficult to imagine a highly orthodox Christian feeling equally sanguine that his truth is only one among a number of equally acceptable religious truths. The first link in our causal chain, then, postulated a high association between Christian orthodoxy and Christian particularism.

The second link follows from the consequences of particularism. For the highly particularistic Christian, religious outsiders--members of other faiths and the irreligious--assume a special

21

saliency and demand a forthright response. The religious outsider cannot simply be ignored. Initially, religious outsiders are likely to generate missionary zeal on the part of the particularistic Christian--a desire to win these "apostates" to the one true faith. When the call to conversion is rejected, however, the hostility latent in particularism is likely to be activated.

This hostility, according to our theory, is capable of being directed against all adamant religious outsiders whether they are of another faith or none. However, in America, the Jews are the most visible religious outsiders. Moreover, from the perspective of the particularist, the Jews more than any other religious group have had the greatest opportunity to know about Christ and to accept him as Savior. Yet, they have rejected him. Some particularistic Christians, we suspected, might be capable of tolerating this ambiguity and be able to contain simmering feelings of hostility. For most, however, we expected that the strain would be too much to bear. Consequently, a strong association was hypothesized between particularism and specifically religious hostility toward Jews.

As to the nature of this hostility, it was expected, of course, that it would be manifested in a perception of the Jews as responsible for the Crucifixion. Most Christians, whether particularistic or not, we felt, probably hold to this image. The difference lies in the interpretation given this view of history. In the eyes of the particularist, we theorized, the Jews remain guilty; the Jews provoked God's wrath by crucifying Jesus, and have suffered under divine judgment ever since. Their tribulations will not cease until they extirpate their guilt by accepting Salvation through Christ. Less orthodox and less particularistic Christians, on the other hand, might not be expected to draw this link between the ancient and the modern Jews, and thus not be armed with religious predilections to discredit the Jews.

Orthodoxy, then, we postulated, is likely to lead to particularism which, in turn, is likely to produce religious hostility toward the Jews. The last link in our causal chain is secular anti-Semitism, and here we expected that religious hostility toward Jews would spill over into a propensity to accept negative stereotypes of Jews and to feel hostile toward them on other than purely religious grounds.

Two additional things need to be said about these theoretical ideas before turning to report how we tested them. First, our theory conceived of religious ideology as capable of exercising an independent effect on anti-Semitism. It is not that certain people who are disposed to accept this form of religious ideology are also prone to be anti-Semitic. The religious ideology, our theory asserted, is a cause of anti-Semitism, not simply a corollary of it. Secondly, while we anticipated, of course, that the theory would be confirmed by the empirical data to be collected, we did not predict that it would be found to be particularly potent or widespread.

Armed with out theory, we then proceeded to plan a study to test it. For the present report, we shall not go into detail about our methodology. Those interested will find the details in our book which will be published in the spring of 1966.[1] Suffice to say here that we collected our data from two sources. First, we administered 3,000 lengthy questionnaires, requiring on the average three hours to complete, to a random sample of Protestant and Roman Catholic church members residing in four counties along the western side of San Francisco Bay. Secondly, we retested our theoretical model through 1,976 interviews collected from a national sample of the adult population of the country. In effect, the first data-collection operation enabled us to test our theory in depth in one area of the country. The second was undertaken to check the "generalizability" of our findings for the country as a whole. For practical reasons, we were obliged in the national study to be much more economical in the number of questions asked than in the Bay Area study. However, since the two studies were done serially, we were able in designing the national study to choose the most central questions bearing on our theoretical scheme as these were revealed in the more intensive study.

What, then, did we find? In brief, the data from both of our studies provide strong confirmation of our theoretical model. As expected, orthodoxy is found to be highly associated with particularism. In turn, particularism is found to produce religious hostility toward the Jews. To be sure, nonparticularistic Christians are about as prone as particularistic ones to blame the Jews for the death of Jesus. The difference, as expected, is that the particularists interpret this historical event invidiously and conceive of the modern Jews as still bearing the guilt for the presumed actions of their forebears.

This process--orthodoxy to particularism to religious hostility--culminates, also as expected, in secular anti-Semitism. Almost inexorably, those caught up in this syndrome of religious ideology are led to a more general anti-Semitism. This is true whether anti-Semitism is defined in terms of negative stereotypes or negative feelings toward Jews, or in terms of countenancing hostile acts toward them.

One can never be sure, except when it is possible to adopt the most rigorous experimental design, that a set of relations which appear causal are indeed so. This is a problem, of course, which confronted us in our own inquiry. Our evidence documents without question that religious ideology and anti-Semitism are descriptively related. Is the relationship also causal? Since our study used a survey approach, our answer can only be tentative. However, two pieces of evidence lend considerable support to a conclusion that the relationship is indeed causal, that Christian belief of the kind we have described can and does lead independently to anti-Semitism.

One way that we went about testing for spuriousness was to try to determine whether the religious ideology which we had found so strongly related to anti-Semitism was also related to prejudice against Negroes. It would greatly strengthen our case, we felt, if it could be shown that our model did not similarly predict prejudice against Negroes. The logic of this position may not be immediately apparent, for clearly prejudice against both Jews and Negroes, as well as against other racial and ethnic groups, is very highly correlated. However, we had not been attempting to account for anti-Semitism in general, but to uncover and isolate specifically religious causes for hatred of the Jews. Since Negroes are largely Christians, these same religious factors should not operate to generate hostility toward them. To the degree that we had successfully uncovered purely religious sources of prejudice, our model ought to fail to account for racial prejudice. By and large, this is the thrust of our findings: While religious ideology is massively related to anti-Semitism, it bears no significant relationship to prejudice toward Negroes.

We also tested for spuriousness by systematically examining other possible explanations which could account for our findings. For example, perhaps, we surmised, the relationship is an artifact produced because lower-class persons are more likely to be anti-Semitic and also more likely to be orthodox and particularistic in their religious faith. Religious ideology, therefore, might not be the cause of anti-Semitism. Rather, the two might be related descriptively only because both are caused by social class. Testing for this and a series of other alternative explanations uniformly failed to support them. In every case, religious ideology was found to be independently related to anti-Semitism.

In survey analysis, there is always the possibility that some overlooked factor might explain away a relationship had the investigator been ingenious enough to think of introducing it. We recognized this to be a possibility in our analysis--as in anybody's analysis. We sought to be as rigorous as possible in considering alternative explanations. Within the degree of rigor that we applied, however, we found nothing to suggest that our theoretical model is only descriptively true; all of our evidence suggests that it is causally true as well.

In concluding this brief summary of our study, there are still several important descriptive matters to be reported on. How orthodox are contemporary Christians, and to what extent does orthodoxy lead to particularism? In turn, what is the magnitude of the religious hostility which orthodoxy and particularism produce? And, finally, how much of the total incidence of contemporary anti-Semitism can reasonably be attributed to religious sources?

Answers to these questions require a full explication of how our various concepts were "operationalized" and a detailed discussion of how we defined anti-Semitism. It has taken us over 250 pages in our book to deal with these matters, and we are obliged, therefore, to refer you to the book for detailed answers to these questions.

In short compass, we can report that the problem is far from being an insignificant one. By a very conservative estimate, it would appear that no less than one-fourth of American anti-Semitism is attached to religious sources. In terms of absolute numbers rather than percentages, our data indicate that the anti-Semitism of at least 17.5 American Christians is rooted in their religious faith.

What concerns us now is that our findings be faced honestly and acted upon constructively. If we only produce an outrage-- perhaps because in pursuing the sources of anti-Semitism we are perceived as having carelessly trod on sacred ground and as having been insensitive to matters which are, for many, the keystone of their lives--then we shall have failed. At the same time, unless we provoke significant concern among Christians, we shall also have accomplished nothing.

We recognize that the issues raised by the study are both sensitive and difficult. All humane men would agree that an end to anti-Semitism ought to be passionately sought. Yet few Christians could agree to sacrifice their faith for such a cause. Herein lies the dilemma, and indeed the challenge, of our findings. Is traditional Christian orthodoxy incompatible with Christ's teaching of brotherhood? The modern Christian answer, it seems to us, ought to be that no faith incompatible with love and brotherhood can possibly be called Christian. Yet not only our own findings, but centuries of history, reveal the difficulty in Christianity of making love triumph over self-righteousness and of reconciling what people espouse with what they do.

Until the process by which religion fosters anti-Semitism has been abolished, the Christian conscience must bear the guilt of bigotry. Even then, the moral duty of Christians, and of us all, remains clear: to oppose intolerance and prejudice where they are found until we finally learn to love one another.

---

[1] Charles Y. Glock and Rodney Stark, Christian Beliefs and Anti-Semitism. New York: Harper and Row, 1966.

THREE

Anti-Semitism in America today

A. Abbot Rosen
Midwest Director
Anti-Defamation League of B'nai B'rith

It is not the purpose of this paper to explore the historic roots of anti-Semitism. The religious factor is being examined by the participants in this conference. Dr. Charles Glock and his colleagues at the University of California, in their program of publications based upon their studies, will provide many of the insights which we lack concerning the psychological and socio-economic roots of present-day anti-Semitism. Rather is this a brief description of American anti-Semitism in its impacts on the lives of five and one-half million Americans of the Jewish faith and, conversely, on the lives of the vast majority of their fellow Americans with whom they interact daily.

One can readily affirm the positives in American Jewish life in a society in which the vast majority are of other faiths. Never in the history of the dispersion of the Jewish people has a Jewish community achieved an economic, social or political status which surpasses that of the present-day American Jewish community. Jews share in the good life of our affluent society. They have the opportunity to practice their religion freely, to support their families, to educate their children, and to participate fully in the political process. America has fulfilled the high hopes and expectations of the Jewish immigrant forefathers who, fleeing from tyranny, came to this promised land of freedom. Jews have achieved distinction in the arts, sciences and professions, in business and government, far beyond their dreams.

Extremist anti-Semitism on an organized and effective basis, the type with which we were familiar in this country in the 1930's and which in its ultimate form resulted in Europe in the extermination of six million of our fellows, is no longer a significant factor on the American scene. We have the Radical Right, which is in certain respects antithetical to the values which underlie the safety and security of Jews and other minority groups in this country. But this movement is a threat to American democracy generally and not specifically anti-Semitic. We even have a tiny handful in the netherworld of our society which would emulate Adolph Hitler, but for all practical purposes the effective anti-Semitic professional bigot has a miniscule place in the American scheme of things.

It is when we look to the practices of the good and polite people in our society, the folks who have been dubbed "the gentle people of prejudice," that we realize we have still a long road to travel before the American Jew is truly and completely rid of the badges of inferiority which were first imposed upon him in European society and later conveyed to American shores.

These are some of the specifics. For a decade the Anti-Defamation League office in Chicago has surveyed the extent of discrimination against Jews in the purchase and rental of homes in our North suburban communities. These surveys are readily accomplished because the realtors circulate to each other the listings of properties for sale at any particular time. In their descriptions of these properties they will indicate which should not be offered to Jews for sale or rent. The percentages of such restricted listings will vary from community to community, with some completely closed to Jews, others open in part or only in certain areas. Overall and consistently, approximately one of three of these properties are closed, are unavailable for sale or rent to a Jewish family.

28

This does not mean that Jews are underhoused, that they are forced to live in inferior surroundings, as are certain other minorities who face housing discrimination. For the Jew there is the opportunity to move around these barriers and into a neighborhood which wants him. But it is appalling to think that there are hundreds of thousands of residents in this area and millions in the country who live in neighborhoods which are walled off from Jews. This situation may stem from attitudes of residents, or from the actions of real estate dealers which may not represent the wishes of homeowners. Regardless of the cause, the fact remains that this policy of exclusion is widespread.

From general observation we can conclude that Jews are sharing in the general American prosperity. This is explained in part by statistics indicating that in the last two generations Jews have achieved more higher education than the population in general. (This relationship between higher education and income also pertains to certain of the Protestant denominations.) But this picture is marred by the denial of equal opportunity for Jews in many segments of our economic society. Several years ago here in Chicago, before the fair employment practices law barred the keeping of discriminatory records, ADL examined the job orders received by commercial employment agencies for stenographers and other female clerical help. In Chicago's Loop some 30% of such positions were automatically barred to Jewish girls, and this in a period of grave shortage of persons with these skills.

Two years ago ADL completed a study of white-collar and executive employment of the Big Three motor companies in Detroit. It was found that of 51,000 persons so employed, only 300 were Jews--a minute 1% of this type of employment. In this major American industry Jews have but an insignificant role. This is the essence of the problem.

A study of an American public utility with which we all do business every day indicates that of its executive echelons totalling 1,100 employees, only 1% are Jewish. The « Harvard Business Review » for March-April of this year estimates that less than 1% of the executive personnel in heavy industry are Jews, while 8% of all college graduates are Jewish. There are many and complex reasons for this phenomenon of the absence of Jews from certain sectors of American industry which cannot be examined in detail here. But investigations do indicate that an important factor to explain this meager representation is discrimination, past and--hopefully to a lesser degree--present.

Social discrimination (that is, discrimination by private and service clubs) provides another measure of the length of the road which Jews must still travel to be fully accepted. Students of the American social scene believe that the exclusion of Jews from the downtown club and the country club is an expression not only of social snobbism but at times even represents an attempt by its practitioners to hold economic, political and other advantages which they might not otherwise possess.

If the power structure in any community discriminates against Jews, the resultant practices will tend to be adopted by the community generally. The industrialist will be confirmed in his negative view about Jewish plant managers; the plant managers in turn will find it more expedient not to employ Jewish subordinates. Lower-echelon civic groups, imitative as they are of social "leaders," will find sanction for similar exclusions. The university, upon whose board of trustees sit members of the discriminatory club, will not protest a quota system; the fraternities will mimic their elders in exclusionary practices. Thus may a new generation, while still in its formative years, be schooled in the ways and benefits of discrimination.

Exclusion from social clubs is the aspect of discrimination against Jews which is most pervasive in American life. Our studies indicate that 67% of American clubs practice religious discrimination. If the thesis is accepted that many of these clubs are factors in the structures which influence political and economic life in their communities, then this discrimination has serious implications for the Jewish present and future.

Parenthetically, a consequence of the development of the institution of the Christian club has been the emergence of the Jewish club. This represents a further institutionalization of religious separatism which does not bode well for the efforts of those who would recognize religious differences on the American scene only when pertinent, as in the house of worship. There is hardly anything "Christian" or "Jewish" about a vast majority of our private and social and service clubs in America. Perhaps in many instances, quite the contrary.

In some areas of social concern, particularly in public accommodations and higher education in its various ramifications, our problems have been greatly diminished.

It was not too many years ago that the American resort hotel, in boasting of its attractions, noted the absence of Jews from its clientele. The typical slogan in the resort brochure or newspaper advertisement proclaimed that "Churches are nearby."

Very rarely was this meant to signal that Sunday worship was convenient and encouraged. Rather did it indicate that Jews were unwelcome. Today, probably as much the result of economics and legislation as quickening American conscience, relatively few hotels boast as freely of the absence of Jews as they do of the quality of their accommodations and cuisine. Statistics show that as recently as 1958 one out of four American resorts did not welcome Jews; five years later this ratio had dropped to one in ten. With the passage of federal legislation outlawing such discrimination, this problem promises to be fully resolved in the near future.

But it is in the area of higher education that the most spectacular gains have been made in reducing the barriers against Jews. In the recent past the numerus clausus or percentage restriction on admission of Jews to college, graduate and professional school was a fact of American life. The Jewish applicant for admission had to meet not only the normal requirements, such as good academic performance and promise, but would have to fit himself within a rigid quota for members of his group. There was the phenomenon, for instance, of a large number of American Jews receiving their medical degrees in foreign lands, even though their no more talented peers--non-Jews--found admission to American medical schools. It was after World War II that the American educational establishment took hold in a number of historic conferences and pronouncements and established the proposition that American higher education should be offered on an equal basis, regardless of creed or race. Now rare is the case where Jewish boys or girls are confronted with the type of discrimination which their parents took very much for granted-- and, indeed, thought little about challenging, so intrinsic was it to "the American way of life." The ≪ Harvard Business Review ≫ of this month estimates that 25% of the graduates of Ivy League colleges are Jewish. What a long road we have traveled from the time when some presidents of these institutions would not only freely proclaim the existence of religious quotas but justify them.

This brief account of anti-Semitism in America has dealt primarily with overt manifestations of prejudice. Not much attention has been given to the extent of hostile beliefs and feelings about Jews. While there is evidence that attitudes toward Jews have improved in recent years, there still remains a massive amount of anti-Jewish feeling in American society. The findings of the Survey Research Center of the University of California indicate the prevalence of widely held hostile beliefs about Jews.

A substantial proportion of the American population subscribes to anti-Jewish beliefs, and this constitutes a reservoir of prejudice which always poses a potential danger. Discrimination, the acting out of prejudices, has obviously decreased substantially. The case is neither so obvious nor certain with regard to the level of prejudice--which is very much harder to measure. Research does indicate that anti-Jewish feelings are extensive, and as long as these exist, the danger of the transition from attitude to action is ever present.

It is hoped that the seminarians who are being trained in their institutions to assume pastoral duties will accept as part of the burden of their ministries the countering of the secular as well as the theological misconception of the Jew; that they will urge the practice of the same love for the individual Jew as they would wish for themselves; that they accept him as a good neighbor and a good friend. When Christian and Jew share the American experience more fully, they enrich their own lives, they prepare a finer legacy for their children.

FOUR

Christian ethnocentrism: a climate for anti-Semitism?

Donald R. Campion, S.J.
Associate Editor, America

I should begin by protesting that my position as author of this paper is somewhat less than enviable. My contribution to this conference, as I see it, is rather much that of a middleman. The area I have been asked to explore lies in between the domain of the sociologist and that of the theologian. That means, in a sense, I may simply expose myself to fire from both sides. What I propose to do, in any event, is to set forth a certain number of points for general reflection on the nature of ethnocentrism. Then I hope to indicate areas that I judge merit closer consideration, particularly by those who have responsibility in Christian seminaries for curriculum, religious-education programs, and the like.

At the outset, I wish to sound a note of caution about the ambiguity in the concept of ethnocentrism. The word itself is one we have received, for better or worse, from the sociologists. It was William Graham Sumner, a founding father of American sociology, who coined the usage we have today. My intention is not to deny its usefulness as a tool for sociologists and others, but to point up problems that its use poses. My uneasiness concerns certain overtones or undercurrents associated with this use. These, I suggest, can force one into unnecessarily difficult and misleading stands.

There is, chiefly, the unspoken belief that to be ethnocentric is automatically to be morally bad. Inevitably, then, all of us experience moments of guilt for traces of ethnocentrism relating to national background or what-have-you. Yet, we ask, is it really necessary to feel guilty about normal manifestations of patriotism or other positive sentiments? Should not, moreover, the same question apply to positive awareness of identification with a religious group? In other words, ought we not to start with a "neutral" conception of ethnocentrism as such? It would be unfortunate to begin our discussions with an assumption that there is something wrong with enjoying a sense of security based on awareness of belonging to a particular religious group. If our understanding of ethnocentrism involves such an assumption, it is my impression that this is so because of a basic ambiguity in the definition of the term. This ambiguity is not wholly absent even from the writings of a man like Sumner, whose primary interest is that of a sociologist confronting a social phenomenon.

In his classic « Folkways » (1907), a "study of the sociological importance of usages, manners, customs, morals, and mores," Sumner tells us that ethnocentrism is the technical name for the "view of things in which one's own group is the center of everything, and all others are scaled and rated with reference to it." As a consequence, "each group nourishes its own pride and vanity, boasts itself superior, exalts its own divinities, and looks with contempt on outsiders." The problem with all this is that we simply do not know from Sumner whether he thought that the elements of prejudice, bigotry, hostility and contempt he thus links to the ethnocentric attitude were inevitable components of ethnocentrism as such. In other words, did he conceive of <u>negative</u> ethnocentrism as necessary for group survival and the preservation of "folkways"?

When one reads Sumner on "sentiments in the in-group and towards the out-groups," his position remains ambiguous. "The relation of comradeship and peace in the we-group and that of hostility and war towards other-groups," he writes, "are correlative to each other." My own interpretation of Sumner's meaning coincides with that of Robin M. Williams, Jr., in his ≪ Strangers Next Door ≫ (1964). Williams notes that Sumner says simply "are correlative" rather than "necessarily occur together." More importantly, since our primary concern here is not the exegesis of early sociological texts, "the consensus of studies," as Williams further remarks, "seems to be that continued interaction between culturally distinctive peoples need not result in conflict."

My reason for belaboring this point is that confusion on it has hampered intelligent discussion and study of ethnocentrism, particularly when the specific area of concern is that of relations among religious groups. Some who approach the question from the vantage point of the social sciences have done so with at least an implicit preconception that ethnocentrism here must inevitably issue in contempt and hostility. Others, taking their point of departure from a theological platform about which they may harbor some personal sense of insecurity, have shared this conviction and judged that the topic was too explosive to explore in depth. In the latter instance, serious examination of such matters may seem to involve the threat of raising potentially embarrassing questions, some even threatening the religious commitment itself. Can one be strong in one's own faith, the troubling doubt runs, without maintaining a hostile posture with respect to the "other" present in the person of the heretic, the unbeliever or theological outsider?

It should be obvious from the foregoing why I must be unhappy about an unqualified statement such as that of Daniel J. Levinson in his study of ethnocentric ideology in ≪ The Authoritarian Personality ≫ (1950): "Ethnocentrism is based on a pervasive and rigid ingroup-outgroup distinction; it involves stereotyped negative imagery and hostile attitudes regarding outgroups, stereotyped positive imagery and submissive attitudes regarding ingroups, and a hierarchical, authoritarian view of group interaction in which ingroups are rightly dominant, outgroups subordinate."

I have similar difficulty with Bernhard E. Olson, author of the careful study on ≪ Faith and Prejudice ≫ (1963), when he writes elsewhere: "Ethnocentrics, unlike anti-ethnocentrics, cannot love their own groups without expressing antipathy toward others. They draw sharp lines of exclusion, and reject and downgrade the outgroup in various ways."[1]

All this qualification is not to deny, however, the too evident and all too lamentable fact that history--both distant and near--

35

is filled with instances of religious ethnocentrism that actually gave rise to bigotry, hatred and violent expressions of fear or contempt. One must agree with Milton Rokeach when he writes, in his article on "Paradoxes of Religious Belief" in the January-February 1965 issue of « Trans-action », that man has "committed some of the most horrible crimes and wars in the holy name of religion." Surely, no generation of Christians in history has had more reason to concur in that judgment that one which bears living memory of obscene efforts in Nazi Germany or apartheid South Africa to justify unthinkable inhumanity in the name of a Gospel of love.

It is one thing to insist, as I do, that ethnocentrism is at root a "neutral" concept, and that Christian ethnocentrism, specifically, need not involve prejudice, hostility or contempt toward non-Christians and, in particular, Jews. It is another to recognize clearly and without cavil that Christian ethnocentrism has assured hideous forms and shapes, and that it can prove to be a climate for anti-Semitism. Our task in this colloquium is, I take it, to inquire how such things could happen and to discuss means of preventing their recurrence. My starting point is much the same as that set forth some years ago by Dr. John C. Bennett, now president of Union Theological Seminary in New York, at a conference on a similar theme. He said: "It seems to me that we are dealing with a deep and pervasive tendency in a culture influenced by the Christian-Jew contrast and that even when there is little explicit religious anti-Judaism among Christians, there is a religious conditioning of Christians and, more broadly, of Gentiles who are influenced by Christianity and who think of themselves as 'belonging to a Christian majority,' which prepares them for a negative attitude toward Jews."

On that occasion, Dr. Bennett went on to add: "The main theme of my comment is that, while Christian teaching does contain elements which stimulate anti-Jewish prejudice, it does have within itself the needed antidotes for this prejudice." In a companion study prepared for the same conference, I insisted that "each of the major traditions cherishes among its most fundamental tenets a set of absolutes which are at odds with the bigotry we associate with the ethnocentric personality."[2]

Mention of the "ethnocentric personality" should remind us that we are dealing with a highly complex sociological and psychological phenomenon. This essay will make no pretense of entering on an analysis of the narrowly psychological aspects of personality structure or dynamics that may play a part in the growth of anti-

Semitism in an individual who happens to be a Christian. My concern is rather with the theological and, more immediately, with the religio-sociological origins and implications of Christian ethnocentrism.

To what extent or in what sense, I ask, does Christian ethnocentrism prove to be a climate for anti-Semitism? Is there something intrinsic to Christian theology or the sociology of the Christian community that positively contributes to the formation of anti-Semitic attitudes? Is there some inevitable reason why Christianity has, on occasion, failed to provide an antidote against the pathological emergence of such attitudes among its communicants? Are there elements in the Christian faith and order that too easily lend themselves to use as a "cover" or pretext for anti-Semitism, even when the root "cause" of anti-Semitism lies elsewhere?

Robin Williams, in « Strangers Next Door », offers us a convenient checklist of factors that may explain an outbreak of what I prefer to call negative ethnocentrism or ethnocentric prejudice and discrimination. He suggests that one examine: (1) the nature of the social system itself within which the two groups exist or find themselves; (2) the extent to which one group is (or, as W. I. Thomas and others have reminded us, is seen as) a threat to the other; (3) elements of understanding or misunderstanding between groups. Let me indicate briefly how these factors could prove operative in the outbreak of Christian ethnocentric prejudice against Jews or Judaism.

(1) When Williams speaks of the significance of the social system itself, he refers to a situation in which prejudice comes to be considered as "normal" in a given society or social context. In other words, we face a situation in which negative attitudes toward the outsider have been built into accepted cultural definitions, etc. At this point, with regard to our concern at this conference, we must turn to the theologian, the biblical scholar or the church historian for light on the sources of a phenomenon such as early Christian anti-Semitism. Equally important is the need to inquire whether certain ways of enunciating otherwise unexceptional theological statements might not occasion or stimulate unsuspected insecurity over the status of Christianity as, say, a "daughter" religion. Could such concern give rise to unconscious resentments against another?

(2) The importance of determining the extent to which one group regards the other as a threat is obvious enough. I use the word "regard" advisedly, since we are dealing with attitudes and here one must reckon with an individual's "definition of the situ-

ation" (to use W. I. Thomas' term) as seriously as one takes into account the concrete or actual situation itself. In the present instance, one might ask under what conceivable title would members of the Christian group--so numerically and institutionally dominant, at least in the West--regard the Jewish community as a threat. Here I incline to the view that we are not dealing with a factor that is immediately or urgently contributory to the genesis of anti-Semitism among Christians. It is interesting to ask, however, whether some manifestations of Christian anti-Semitism in the past did not point to at least the _felt_ presence of a threat troubling the "innovators," one to which some responded by denigrating upholders of the status quo.

(3) At first glance, it might seem that understanding between groups, as such, can never be said to result in prejudice or bigotry. It is helpful, however, to recall in this connection a point made by Williams: "Understanding will reduce antipathy and the likelihood of conflict only if the groups like or respect what they discover by understanding each other or if one group finds that the threat posed by the other, though real, is not so severe, unalterable, or immediate as previously believed." The process of dissipating prejudice through promoting understanding of the other is not helped, certainly, where the process of arriving at understanding remains incomplete. Indeed, in such a situation, we may confront the even greater menace of the bigoted "expert" who judges himself to be fully justified in his contempt of the other and uniquely qualified to propagandize his distorted vision. In some instances, of course, the "expert" will have come to his greater "scientific" understanding of the other-- the Jew in the case of a Christian hatemonger--by seeking a rational defense of an already fully formed prejudice. In others, it may be that tragic misunderstanding has grown out of a limited measure of understanding compounded with external factors that would nourish hostility. In one way or other, we confront the story of anti-Semitism through the centuries.

One thinks here of a remark by Jacob Bernard Agus, in the first volume of his « Meaning of Jewish History », about the "tragic wall of hate which surrounded the Jewish people from the time of their first dispersion." He notes that this "formidable wall of animosity," while "not unmingled with admiration and even awe, was unique in that an ideological dimension and several special motivations were added to the 'normal' hates that divide mankind." He further reminds us:

Even before the rise of Christianity, anti-Semitism had become an intellectualized hate, almost an ideology. Its bill of complaint ran about as follows: the most odious of all peoples; they hate all men and consider it sinful to do a favor to pagans; they scorn and insult the gods; they treat all non-Jews as "unclean"; they seek special exemptions for themselves from the laws to which all others are subject; they look forward to the ultimate subjection of the rest of mankind; they do not want to cultivate fraternal ties with any people, preferring to live in an isolated enclave of their own.[3]

These charges, Professor Agus rightly notes, "are essentially the arguments of the classical anti-Semites." For the Christian, even today, there is a bitter ring to the truth of this remark, since such accusations--embellished at times with a sophisticated fringe of learned citations--still come from those who should know much better. There is for the Christian of today the added irony, when one of his fellows makes such charges, that the same accusations, in other times and under other circumstances, have been directed against the members of their own community of faith. It should not be difficult to imagine how simply a Christian educator might make this very point in an attempt to forewarn his students against anti-Semitism in any form.

In thus briefly outlining some factors that may give rise to negative ethnocentrism in the Christian, I do not wish to leave the impression that I believe the task of dealing with such ethnocentrism where it exists is an easy one. Commenting on the curious link between religion and prejudice, Gordon Allport wrote in « The Nature of Prejudice » (1954) that "the chief reason why religion becomes the focus of prejudice is that it usually stands for more than faith--it is the pivot of the cultural tradition of a group." Thus, one seeking to prevent or to combat a phenomenon such as Christian anti-Semitism must be prepared to do battle with a Hydra. In some instances, perhaps, where a head has been lopped off, one will find, as William James once remarked, that "piety is the mask, the inner face is tribal instinct." Our primary concern in this matter, to be sure, must be to eliminate anything in the life of the Christian community at large that would contribute to contempt for or hatred of Jews. But it would be irresponsible to limit our attention to the specifically religious or theological field in seeking to uproot anti-Semitism.

To combat negative ethnocentrism in this or any other form is not, of course, to weaken commitment to one's own faith. For both Jew and Christian, religious commitment is linked with a sense of identity in a group--the People of God. This sense of identity can and must be fostered without fear of generating hurtful sentiments against outsiders. Indeed, as Bernard D. Weinryb, author of a study on the intergroup content of Jewish religious textbooks, once observed: "Cultivation of patriotism and self-esteem of a minority which is usually relegated to an inferior status in larger society is bound to save the minority from rejection and self-hatred." Under such circumstances, Weinryb argued, "one is even justified in theorizing that in a minority situation ingroup 'ethnocentrism' may work to alleviate prejudice toward outgroups."[4]

Indeed, there is evidence that indicates the truly or interiorly committed believer will be less readily open to religious prejudice than one whose commitment is more external in nature or less interiorized. Reporting in « The Nature of Prejudice » on studies made of groups of Protestant and Catholic laymen, Allport tells us that "in both studies the same result occurred: those who were considered the more devout, more personally absorbed in their religion, were far less prejudiced than the others." He added: "The institutional type of attachment, external and political in nature, turns out to be associated with prejudice." Other studies on tendencies or predispositions toward prejudice in religiously differentiated groups have underlined the importance of this distinction between one whose religious convictions relate to an internalization of his church's central teaching or moral precepts and one whose allegiance--though perhaps seemingly more rigid--is chiefly external in character.

Olson's study of Protestant catechetical materials revealed there is no inevitable link between what might be called full theological orthodoxy and negative ethnocentrism. It will be recalled that he divided the materials in his survey into four categories: fundamentalist, conservative, neoorthodox and liberal. He showed that a "neo-orthodox curriculum with a biblical approach is equally capable with liberalism of taking a generally high outlook toward all outside groups."[5] On a more generalized plane, I have long felt that there is a great deal of meaning in a remark of Etienne Gilson in his essay on « Dogmatism and Intolerance »: "There is no necessary connection between philosophical dogmatism and political tyranny, no more than there is between philosophical skepticism and political liberty. . . . Like any other moral vice, intolerance is a sin against the very nature of reason and one of the worst among the countless forms of stupidity. But precisely because intellectual light is his only weapon, a true philosopher cannot afford to be a skeptic with regard to the fundamental principles of human life."[6]

This sort of philosophical reflection I would extend to the concern each religious group may entertain for certain values it judges to be of transcending importance. My guess is that both Christian and Jew would feel perfectly free to insist that a limited form of religious intransigence, if not apparent intoler- ance, is legitimate in some instances. One such would be when confronted by a question along the lines of that raised by Milton Rokeach in an article cited earlier in this essay: "From the standpoint of democracy," he asked, "is it desirable to have a society in which everyone marries only within his own sect or denomination?" It may well be that most Christians and Jews would find themselves arriving at roughly the same value judg- ment on such an issue.

In the closing portion of this paper, I would like briefly to deal with the specific problem of the responsibility incumbent on Christian seminaries to face up to the possibilities and reali- ties of Christian ethnocentrism precisely insofar as it may be a climate for anti-Semitism. Olson, I believe, has given us many helpful leads in this area. He observed--with reason, in my opinion--that "since Judaism, as such, is not seen as presenting any great threat to Christian freedom and responsibility in Amer- ican society, it appears that, for curriculum writers, the main problems with respect to Jews and Judaism are exegetical and expositional."[7]

I would add to Olson's remark only the comment that it applies to religion teachers and preachers as well as to authors and scholars. There remains, moreover, the problem of potential conflict arising out of a preoccupation with Judaism, not as a theological threat, but as the embodiment of social values seem- ingly at variance with those of a particular Christian group. I am thinking here of the sort of public conflict that can develop over issues of public policy such as the question of prayers in public schools. There is much that can and should be done in the way of interpreting to members of other religious groups the precise grounds on which a group takes its stand on such an issue. It is important, furthermore, that all necessary distinc- tions be made between the doctrinal bases for a particular stand and the bases which may lie in varying judgments on the social context and what it portends for the group. Here we enter into the complicated area of differences in past historical experience and present preoccupations of different groups, differences that can be significant even where there may be a large area of agreement among them on religious doctrinal matters.

Olson is surely right when he calls attention to his research finding that "the most favorable portraits of the Jews as a whole are made by those communicators whose writings show that they are most aware of the Jews as a continuing people, living among Christians, to whom Christians owe a spiritual debt, and one they are obligated to treat with consideration and fairness."[8] It will be obvious to anyone familiar with the contents of the Declaration on Non-Christian Religions discussed and approved in principle at the third session of the Second Vatican Council in the fall of 1964 that the most authoritative guidelines Roman Catholic religious educators and authors have for the drafting of catechetical and homiletic materials is fully in this positive spirit. "With a grateful heart," the declaration states, "the Church of Christ acknowledges that, according to God's saving design, the beginnings of her faith and her election were already among the patriarchs, Moses, and the prophets. . . . The Church, therefore, cannot forget that she received the revelation of the Old Testament from the people with whom God in His ineffable mercy concluded the former Covenant. Nor can she forget that she feeds upon the roots of that cultivated olive tree into which the wild shoots of the Gentiles have been grafted (cf. Rom. 11:17-24)." With all this in mind, the document continues to affirm: "Since the spiritual patrimony common to Christians and Jews is of such magnitude, this Sacred Synod wants to support and recommend their mutual knowledge and respect, a knowledge and respect that are the fruit, above all, of biblical and theological studies as well as of fraternal dialogues." For this reason, the conciliar declaration urges upon all members of the Catholic community: "May all, then, see to it that in their catechetical work or in their preaching of the word of God they do not teach anything that could give rise to hatred or contempt of Jews in the hearts of Christians."

In general, following on the statement of the ecumenical council's draft, I place great hope in the powerful impact of contemporary biblical scholarship one encounters in religious circles today. In his latest work, « We Jews and Jesus » (1965), the provost of Hebrew Union College, Samuel Sandmel, testified that he knows of "no area where anti-Jewish feeling, both toward Jews and toward Judaism, is now so rare as it is in the domain of Christian Bible scholars." It is surely not too much to expect that this climate will be transmitted to other circles as these scholars continue to exercise their influence on Christian theology as a whole.

Even the question of presenting the crucifixion narrative and the related issue of the deicide or "Christ-killer" charge against Jews need not unduly worry us. With regard to Protestant religious education, let me cite once more from Olson on this point. "Our finding was that lessons on the crucifixion can produce both positive and negative images of Jews, depending upon the perspectives from which crucifixion lessons were written." He further insists that "positive scores"--a reference to his research procedure in which he graded Protestant catechetical material positively if it presented other religious groups in a positive fashion--"are possible, not only to those who reject or radically reconstruct many of the New Testament events, but also to those who accept the essential New Testament as valid."9

On this same point, the conciliar declaration referred to above should prove an effective instrument among Roman Catholic educators in combatting even potentially negative attitudes. I am personally satisfied that the great majority of American Catholics have been honestly surprised and confused by the widespread discussion of the deicide charge over the course of the sessions of the Second Vatican Council. They had no recollection of ever hearing such a charge made or suggested by any teacher or companion in their personal experience as members of the Catholic community, as students or communicants in Catholic schools or churches. In this respect, their experience paralleled that discovered among New York parochial school youngsters some years ago by Sister Mary Jeanine in her Catholic University study on « Categorical Valuation of Jews Among Catholic Parochial School Children » (1950). Despite these findings, I share the urgent conviction of the American Roman Catholic hierarchy and that of Catholic bishops in many other parts of the world that the Vatican Council should utilize the weight of its authority to denounce any and all monstrous perversions of central Christian beliefs that could engender hatred or contempt for the Jews. As the draft declaration approved by the council in its test vote of November 20, 1964 stated: "May they [teachers and preachers] never present the Jewish people as one rejected, cursed, or guilty of deicide. All that happened to Christ in His passion cannot be attributed to the whole people then alive, much less to that of today. Besides, the Church has always held and holds now that Christ underwent His passion and death freely, because of the sins of all men and out of infinite love."

Two tasks, then, face the Christian educator at every level, from Sunday school, through seminary and college classroom, to the graduate theological seminar: 1) to expose or counteract any alleged "theological" bases for negative ethnocentrism, particularly with regard to Judaism because of the special dangers experienced in this area; 2) to stress, at every level, those elements of Christian faith that can provide the most effective antidotes to anti-Semitism or negative ethnocentrism of any form. In conclusion, I would stress the importance of defining with new clarity one's ultimate goal in religious education. What conception does the educator--be he in seminary, Sunday school, pulpit or theology classroom--have of the finished product for which he labors, the religiously educated and motivated man or woman? The reason for my concern on this score traces back to what the psychologist has to tell us about the fundamental importance-- in areas going far beyond the provision of correctives against prejudice--of furnishing the student of religious faith with a solid sense of security rooted in a strongly positive sense of identity as a member of a particular believing and worshiping community. In the process of achieving that goal, it is my firm belief that genuine religion will be well served, and an effective check provided against that "tribal instinct" which so often lies at the root of religious negative ethnocentrism.

1 Bernhard E. Olson, "Intergroup Relations in Protestant Teaching Materials," Religious Education 55 (March-April 1960) 132-38.

2 Presentations at inauguration of Institute of Human Relations, at headquarters of American Jewish Committee, New York City, January 29, 1960.

3 Jacob Bernard Agus, The Meaning of Jewish History. New York: Abelard-Schuman, 1963. Vol. I, p. 201. (Reprinted by permission of Abelard-Schuman, Ltd. All Rights Reserved 1963 by Jacob Bernard Agus.)

4 Bernard D. Weinryb, "Intergroup Content in Jewish Religious Textbooks," Religious Education 55 (March-April 1960) 109-16.

5 Olson, "Intergroup Relations."

6 Quoted from monograph published by Rutgers University Press, 1952.

7 Olson, "Intergroup Relations."

8 Ibid.

9 Ibid.

FIVE

Reflections on the Ecumenical Council: a Protestant view

Jerald C. Brauer

Dean and Professor of Church History
The Divinity School, University of Chicago

There are many things that might be said concerning the Second Vatican Council. So much has been written, a wide variety of analyses have been made, and countless lectures have been de-livered; therefore, it is exceedingly difficult to determine what might be said in the short space allotted. However, one question is of the utmost significance to the entire dialogue situation, and that is whether or not renewal is actually underway within the Roman Catholic Church.

The last forty-eight hours of the third session, in part, re-formulated this question with great urgency. Moreover, all those interested in dialogue between Roman Catholics, Protestants, and Jews cannot avoid raising the question in light of the dynamics of the Council itself. The checkered history of the statement on the Jews, the difficulties of preparing and finding an acceptable statement on religious liberty, and the general maneuvering within the Council itself make this issue central. The slowness with which some of the bishops have moved in implementing the liturgical reforms of the Council, the reluctance of churchmen-- Protestant, Catholic, and Jewish--to move ahead in dialogue, all make critical the question of the actuality of renewal. Even in the United States a movement opposing the liturgical reforms has developed and become vociferous. Many Protestants think that the entire effort at renewal as expressed by the Second Vatican Council is merely a psychological trick and a vast hoax to fool Protestants. And a number of Roman Catholics are sufficiently distressed by the spirit and actions of the Second Vatican Council that they appear ready to dig in their heels and refuse to move another inch in the direction of renewal pointed by the Council itself.

It is the view of this observer that not only is renewal underway in the Roman Catholic Church, but it is underway at a depth and at a speed that nobody could have predicted four to five years ago. One of the problems confronting Protestants and Jews is that they frequently demand renewal as defined and interpreted from their own point of view. They appear unwilling to allow renewal to occur within the Roman Catholic Church on its own terms, in its own dynamics, and at its own pace. The fact is, Roman Catholicism is not about to become Protestantism and will not proceed with renewal along lines that make sense from the perspective of Protestant history and concepts. To understand the actuality of renewal within the Roman Catholic Church, one must understand it in the context of the history of Roman Catholicism and within the context of the special dynamics and processes peculiar only to Roman Catholicism. When viewed from this perspective, it can easily be seen that renewal is underway, and that it is underway at a depth and a speed that is nothing less than astonishing.

In a brief presentation of this type, one has the possibility to document such a generalization only by quickly recounting several points. Five major assertions will easily demonstrate the presence and the ongoing reality of renewal within the Roman Catholic Church as carried through by the Second Vatican Council.

The first point to be made involves the accomplishments of the Second Vatican Council up through its third session. Three of the four schemata adopted and promulgated are of the utmost importance for the entire history of the Christian Church, and are probably the most important things to occur in the history of the Church since the Reformation itself. The effects of the schema on liturgical reform are the most wide reaching and touch most directly the individual lives of faithful Roman Catholics. The same can be said about this schema in relationship to non-Roman Catholics. Laymen who know little or care less about theological formulations are usually concerned about and can react to changes and forms in worship. Nobody can deny that renewal as expressed by liturgical reform is well underway. Even those Protestants most deeply suspicious of Roman Catholicism cannot ignore or overlook that fact.

Two schemata adopted during the third session will undoubtedly prove to be two of the most important doctrinal statements in modern Roman Catholicism and in modern Church history. The first, « De Ecclesia », sets forth the role, the rights, the function, and the power of the bishops in with and under the pope. In a very profound sense it seeks to complete the work of Vatican I, which had an opportunity to deal only with corollary functions of the papacy. « De Ecclesia » deals with many other exceedingly important issues, but probably this will prove in time to be the most important single issue.

Equally exciting from the point of view of renewal is the schema on ecumenicity, laying down the ground rules for the ecumenical participation of Roman Catholicism with Protestantism and Orthodoxy. For the first time Protestant Churches are actually referred to as Churches, and the implication is no longer that they are separated brethren who, as individuals, might accidentally have become Christian or, through intent, are actually Christian though not in the true Church. It is now stated that within Protestant Churches there remains residual truth through Scripture and the sacraments of baptism and the Lord's Supper. Five years ago statements such as these would have been utterly impossible, and many Protestants still cannot believe what they read. However, these are not idle words; they have been worked out carefully and thoughtfully, and the mind of the Roman Catholic Church was expressed on these points by a vast majority vote.

One could argue that these are but doctrinal statements that remain to be actualized. That is in a sense true, but that is precisely the way history operates. The Church must first express its mind on these issues and then, as history provides the opportunity, actualize the truth step by step. Thus it is unfair to say that renewal is not yet underway because the various points within « De Ecclesia » and « De Ecumeniso » have not yet been implemented or realized. The groundwork has been laid, a new direction has been established, and the Church slowly moves through history. As specific occasions arise, it will act in light of its stand with regard to the Church and ecumenism.

Further evidence of the fact that renewal is actually under-way was provided by the presence of certain theologians at the Council. Many of these theologians had books on the Index ten years ago and were certainly not in favor with the Curia. Key theologians who were suspect only a decade ago now appear to be the major theologians serving as consultants to the bishops and working on the preparation of the various documents. This could not be the case if renewal was not already in midstream. These are the men who are most fully articulating the mind and the heart of the Roman Catholic Church at the present moment in history, and who will provide the leadership as the Church moves ahead.

Thirdly, anybody attending the Council was struck by the con-tent and nature of the interventions and changes proposed at the Council itself. One was impressed by their content, their spirit, their incisiveness, and their vision. The vast majority of the bishops are now well aware of the fact that Pope John XXIII was correct in calling for the "windows of the world to be thrown open" and for the Church to renew itself in order better to serve its Lord. The discussions on poverty, the religious orders, the Church and the world, and marriage revealed the extent to which fresh and exciting thinking is at work within the Church. Any doubts about renewal would be banished upon hearing interventions of this type. This was especially noticeable the day that four cardinals made their famous interventions on the question of marriage and family.

A fourth factor pointing to the reality of renewal was the shift in spirit or outlook that occurred from the first through the third sessions. It was pointed out by the late beloved Cardinal Meyer, as well as by many other American prelates, that this shift from the first through the third sessions was quite evident to most Church fathers. When Pope John first called for a council, nobody knew exactly what he had in mind. In fact, he made clear that as far as he was concerned the Holy Spirit would determine what its eventual direction ought to be. During the first session most of the bishops were uncertain as to why they were there and tended to be quite conservative in outlook. By the second session there was a perceptible shift in the direction of serious efforts of renewal. The so-called conservative bishops found it more and more necessary to explain to a fuller extent why they were taking a particular stand. However, by the time of the third session it was pointed out by many bishops that the shift had taken place. The move for renewal was fully underway, and it was now the

conservatives or those reluctant to change who were forced to
defend the stand they were taking and who found themselves
under constant pressure of those pressing for renewal. This
dynamic rhythm of the Council in itself is a demonstration of
the reality of renewal.

One could give many other reasons for thinking that renewal
is genuine and fully underway; however, for delegated observers
attending the Council, proof was provided by the way they were
received and accepted. Observers were not invited simply to sit
and observe. To be sure, they were not to be given the privilege
of the floor; that would be too much. However, the seriousness
with which their opinions and views were solicited by Roman
Catholic bishops and theologians was proof of the fact that they
were there as more than observers. They were not there as
ornamentation simply to be wined and dined. Observers were
present because Catholic brethren seriously wanted to hear what
they had to say about the key issues that confronted the Church
fathers. Every effort was made to hear from the Protestant and
Orthodox observers both in writing and verbally. Full advantage
was taken of all opportunities by the observers to express their
opinions. More than one observer had the satisfaction of hearing
his views expressed by Roman Catholic bishops and theologians
in the preparation of documents and even from the floor itself.

Thus it is clear from a very brief review of these five points
that renewal is underway, that it is genuine, that it is moving at
a pace none could have predicted. In fact, some think that the
pace is even slightly too fast for many of the Roman Catholic
laity as well as for some of the clergy. This has been true of all
creative moments in history, so one should not be shocked by the
recalcitrance of the minority.

If renewal is a fact and is underway, what does this imply for
the immediate future? Here it is possible for me to speak only from
the viewpoint of Protestantism. First, we are in a totally new
ecumenical age. Once Roman Catholicism entered the ecumenical
picture, the entire situation of dialogue radically altered. The
World Council of Churches has long engaged in ecumenical activities,
and it is more needed than ever before. Nevertheless, until Roman
Catholicism became actively engaged in the ecumenical movement and
in dialogue, the very best efforts of the World Council of Churches
hardly touched the center of the ecumenical impasse. Now, dialogue
in ecumenical activities can never again be carried on the same.
All Churches, all councils of Churches, and especially the World
Council of Churches, have to rethink their nature and their activity.

It can no longer be business as usual! But the implications are not to be felt alone or even primarily at the level of the top echelon. The entrance of Roman Catholicism into ecumenical activity affects every local Roman Catholic, Protestant, and Orthodox parish. Also, it affects the relationship of all of these groups to their Jewish brethren.

The reality of renewal also has vast implications for theologizing and for theological education. It is no longer possible for Roman Catholics, Protestants, or Jews to carry on theology the way they have from the time of the Council of Trent up to Pope John XXIII. All have handled the others as if they did not exist or, at best, as if they were straw men to be destroyed in defense of the truth. No theologian can ever again carry out his systematic effort as if the other traditions did not exist.

Finally, there arises a full set of practical consequences. All religious movements and forces are today confronted with the changed role of religion in relation to a highly successful secular society. This does not mean that they are engaged in common in a crusade against communism or even against secularism. Rather, it means that the religious way of viewing life, its goals, and its meaning is quite different from the non-religious perspective. Implications of this for the basic moral, political, and social questions of our age are profound. It is at this point that the renewal of the Roman Catholic Church and its wholehearted entrance into the ecumenical dialogue will inevitably bring about important changes for all religious faiths. Renewal will bear fruit not only at the theoretical and theological levels, but also at the equally important social-cultural levels. It is then that the actuality and the depth of renewal will be most fully experienced.

SIX

Reflections on the Ecumenical Council: a Jewish view

Joseph L. Lichten
Director, Department of Intercultural Affairs
Anti-Defamation League of B'nai B'rith

Father H. J. Richards began his recent article on "Vatican II and the Jews," published in the English « Clergy Review », with the following story. A Jewish woman heard a priest denouncing the Jews vehemently from the pulpit. She went to see him afterward to complain. He was most apologetic, and assured her that he would not have dreamed of hurting her for the world. "How was I to know," he said, "that there was a Jew in the church?" She replied: "And yet, Father, there was one on the cross."[1]

This story presents the quintessence of the major obstacle blocking the progress of Christian-Jewish rapprochement: there is a habit of anti-Semitic thinking which permeates the fabric of our society.

How destructive this age-old tradition is, does not need to be emphasized. Already in the second century, St. Justin, in his

≪ Dialogue with Trypho ≫, declared that "the tribulations were justly imposed upon [the Jews], because [they] have murdered the Just One." And then came St. Hippolytus, who in his ≪ Demonstratio adversus Judaeos ≫ warned the Jews not to forget that their misfortunes were the result of their having killed Christ, and St. John Chrysostom, who in his ≪ Eight Homilies against the Jews ≫ insisted that, because of the crime of deicide, the Jews would live "under the yoke of servitude without end because God hates the Jews and always hated the Jews."

Writing today, Father Edward H. Flannery, in ≪ The Anguish of the Jews ≫ (1965), says: "After Chrysostom, the theme of deicidal punishment gained wide currency. . . . For centuries it was to supply a pseudo-theological basis for myriad oppressions and degradations of the Jews. On its basis, misguided men considered themselves called to assist the Almighty in effectuating His 'curse' and free to indulge their hostilities with a divine seal of approval." And speaking about most recent times, because of the events of World War II, certain very difficult questions need to be answered. To do this, we must first find the courage and insight to discover the areas where questions should be raised and to phrase the questions themselves.

Some of the most searching inquiries into Christian-Jewish relations are being made today by the Christian churches. The world's attention has been drawn particularly to the Catholic Church, which convened the Second Vatican Ecumenical Council in the fall of 1962. On the last day of its third session, November 20, 1964, the Council adopted a declaration on the attitude of Catholics toward non-Christians, including the Jews. This statement may be considered one of the single most significant events in our common history, because it unequivocally condemns the damaging accusation that has caused the Jewish people such suffering for almost two thousand years: the charge of deicide.

The declaration was drafted in the spirit of the new ecumenism exemplified by the late Pope John XXIII. "I am Joseph, your brother," he said to a delegation of Jewish leaders, and perhaps no pope since Gregory the Great has so amply fulfilled the position of pontifex maximus, or of bridge-builder, toward those of the Jewish faith.

The Protestant churches long ago formulated the basic concept of ecumenism as an instrument for theological progress and unification among themselves. The concept broadened in time, so that it embraced all Christian churches involved in a movement toward unity. But the new ecumenism which Pope John XXIII seemed always to have in mind is broader still. He enlarged both its concept and its approach--the concept to include non-Christians, the approach to include all aspects of human relations. The new ecumenism calls for social justice and intergroup harmony, and not necessarily for unity in religious beliefs and practices; it asks not so much for theological unity as for the unity of human persons; it looks to the welfare of all men of goodwill, not only of Christian peoples. It is a spirit by which people can live not merely alongside each other but with each other. And coming full cycle, the new ecumenism has prompted eminent theologians to reexamine some fundamental issues which previously seemed closed to questions. Ecumenism often is related to the concept of pluralism, as Bishop Blomjous of Tanganyika has so clearly stated:

> We used to think that the Church was sent into the world to gain the adherence of all men to Christ. . . . Today, however, we are faced with the realization that . . . specifically religious pluralism is established in most parts of the world and that the forces of history will eventually make it a universal phenomenon. . . . It seems that religious pluralism is part of God's plan. Can we still assert that the Lord has sent His Church into the world to gather all men in the unity of faith? We are forced to ask ourselves the serious question: What is the theological meaning of religious pluralism? What is God attempting to tell us through the multiplicity of religions?[2]

This broader concept of ecumenism, and its correlation with pluralism, is of great importance and consequence, particularly for our American society. It is still a source of concern, however, to notice in articles and statements made by some Christian leaders a tendency toward the old, narrower treatment of the idea of ecumenism, understood only as a movement toward Christian unity, and not toward mutual understanding and cooperation among all men of goodwill, often regardless of their religious differences.

For all these reasons, the current Ecumenical Council and the declaration on the relationship between the Catholic Church and non-Christian religions is of such great importance. A large part of the Council's value lies in the atmosphere which surrounds it. Its orientation is toward free inquiry, revision, new approaches, aggiornamento and exchanges of views, not only among the bishops themselves on the floor of St. Peter's Basilica but between them and the outside world. As Robert McAffee Brown points out, the great majority of the hierarchy made it apparent that they would welcome comments from outsiders on matters under discussion at the general congregations.[3] Even the diversity of opinion among the Council Fathers was gratifying to see, because the dialogues within St. Peter's encourage dialogues, not just among Catholics, or Catholics and Protestants, but in fact among Christians and non-Christians. Perhaps the importance and the impact of the current Vatican Council rests not only in decrees, schemata, constitutions and declarations but also in the accumulative value of men's minds and hearts, in their warmth and determination to act for the good of all, in the human beings who formed the Ecumenical Council. I include in this impressive human family the official observers. I am particularly happy to share the platform with Dean Brauer today, for he also shared the burden of worry which prevailed during those last weeks of the Third Session. As I recently said at a meeting of Jewish leaders in Chicago, the Protestant observers showed great personal concern and interest in seeing the statement on the Jews voted upon; and on November 20, they expressed deep pleasure about its passage, despite the fact that the statement on religious liberty, so important to them and to all of us, did not reach a vote. For these reasons, although there were no official Jewish observers at the Council, Jews all over the world have been watching its proceedings with interest and involvement.

For this same reason, I have been in Rome on the eve of the First Session and for each of the following two sessions. On my way to Rome, I stopped at Frankfurt for a conference, but I also felt that I had to attend the trials of the Auschwitz murderers. It was a great and painful experience. I sat in the convention hall which was serving as the courtroom, and looked into the faces of some of the men responsible for the death of one-third of the Jewish people. I thought about these accused men, allegedly my fellow human beings, from whom I myself had fled for my life; I thought about the reason for my trip to Europe, which had been the "holocaust kingdom" of six million Jews only twenty years earlier. And I wondered what might have happened if the first Vatican Ecumenical Council of my grandfather's time, 90 years ago, had promulgated a declaration condemning the deicide charge. Would not many have been influenced by the strong moral force which the Church is, and might not many have reached adulthood in the 1930's free from the cancer of anti-Semitism? How many others, still retaining their prejudice and even willing to act upon it violently, might have been restrained by their unprejudiced neighbors?

One of the major purposes of my trip to last fall's convocation in Rome was to present evidence that anti-Semitism in the United States, as elsewhere, is closely linked to the deicide charge. I took with me a most revealing and troubling document dealing with this unfortunate aspect of the American experience. It contained the preliminary findings of a study on religion in American life which is being conducted at the University of California under the sponsorship of the Anti-Defamation League. The decision to examine the possible consequences of church teachings regarding the Jews stemmed from the growing dialogue among both clergy and laity with the Jewish community; Christian churchmen have been concerned by the effect the crucifixion story may have had on the attitudes of many church members. Basically, the study attempted to answer these two questions:

1 Do modern Christians typically blame the historic Jew for the crucifixion?

2 Do these historic images get translated into a picture of the modern Jew as guilty of the alleged crimes of his ancestors?

Of the Catholics in the test group, the study found that 69% believed that Pontius Pilate wanted to spare Jesus from the cross, and 46% believed that the reason Pilate did not succeed was "because a group of powerful Jews wanted Jesus dead"; 61% named the Jews as the group "most responsible for crucifying Christ"; 46% agreed with or were uncertain about the statement that "the Jews can never be forgiven for what they did to Jesus until they accept Him as the true Savior"; and 11% agreed with the statement that "the reason the Jews have so much trouble is because God is punishing them for rejecting Jesus," and 30% were uncertain.

In addition to these questions, there were others concerning stereotypes of Jews--whether they thought themselves "better than other people," whether they were "more likely than Christians to cheat in business," how loyal to America they were and what was their attitude toward Communism. The study found that "Catholics who believed that both ancient and modern Jews were to blame for the crucifixion were much more likely to accept these stereotypes than were Catholics who did not hold such religious opinions."

For the sake of comparison, it must be said that the Protestants in the test group did not fare any better than the Catholics. Breaking the group down into the various denominations, the study revealed that Protestant bodies such as the Episcopalians and the Congregationalists were less likely to hold negative religious images of the Jews than were Catholics. The moderate groups, like the Lutherans, closely paralleled the Catholics, and members of the most fundamentalist churches, such as the Southern Baptists, were much more likely than Catholics to be hostile toward Jews.

In sum, the California study showed that a majority of American Christians interpret the crucifixion story in ways which are not prejudicial to their relations with their Jewish neighbors. Given the concern of the churches to foster ecumenism in the new, broader sense, they can take justifiable pride in the evidence that considerable progress has been made. Nevertheless, a significant minority of American Christians continue to reveal anti-Semitic prejudices, seeing the historic and also the contemporary Jew as responsible for the death of Jesus, and looking upon their Jewish neighbors as somewhat inferior persons according to American standards of upright conduct.

I submitted the findings of the California study to a number of influential American and European Church leaders in Rome, and all of them expressed great interest in the percentages. Arrangements were then made with the Dutch Documentation Center, one of the most respected of the research bureaus preparing background materials for the Council Fathers in Rome, to release the findings. Within two days, a copy of the published summary was placed in the hands of every one of the 2300 bishops and experts present at the Council session. The study was before their eyes ten days prior to the historic debate on the draft declaration on non-Christians. The response to the summary was very rewarding; excerpts were used in official interventions at the Council, in press reports and newscasts, and they continue to appear in print.

The declaration charts a new course for Catholic-Jewish cooperation. Although the document has not yet been promulgated, its adoption has made known the minds of the bishops--minds oriented toward the good, not only of their own Catholic people, but of all men We are indeed now a long way from the Yellow Star of David, the badge of the Jewish outcast. A long road has been traveled from the Fourth Lateran Council of the year 1215, which introduced the badge, to the Second Vatican Council of 1964, with its condemnation of both past and present persecution of the Jewish people.

To a less observant onlooker, it could seem that we have entered an era of unanimous agreement and understanding. But the declaration is not a divining rod, which by a simple pronunciamento could change human hearts and human minds.

Only a few weeks ago, the Italian periodical « La Palestra del Clero» quoted Bishop Luigi Maria Carli, the Italian prelate, as saying:

> I hold it legitimate to be able to affirm that all of the Judaic people of the time of Christ were responsible in solidum for the crime of deicide, even though only the chiefs, followed by a part of the followers, had materially consummated the crime.

> In this very precise sense, and considering the Biblical mentality, even the Judaism of the times after Our Lord participates objectively in the responsibility for the deicide, in the measure in which such Judaism constitutes the free and voluntary continuation of that of those times.[4]

Patriarch Maximos IV Saigh, the Near Eastern prelate, recently elevated to the office of cardinal, stated a month or two ago: "There certainly remains on the forehead of the Jewish people, as long as it is far from Christ the Redeemer, what the prophets of the Old Testament prophesied: a stain of shame. But this stain of shame does not constitute a personal crime. . . . These are essential truths which a reasonable mind cannot deny." The Near Eastern patriarch went even further. He said: "Because of their propaganda skill, the media of which are in their hands and under their influence, the Jews can clothe reality as they wish . . . if the great majority of the Council, and namely the American prelates, voted for the declaration, it is for personal reasons and interests. The personal reasons are dictated by a sentiment of pity due to the massacre of millions of Jews by the Nazis, and the interest is due to the fact that the great number of American [bishops] have commercial interests with Jews."[5]

Patriarch Saigh's communique made a somber impression on the Catholic community in the United States. Monsignor Higgins, of Washington, D.C., answered this attack on the American episcopate by stating: "The latter part of this statement is demonstrably unfair to the American bishops and however unintentionally, is calculated, I am afraid, to fan the flames of anti-Semitism--a monstrous evil which, in all its forms, is solemnly condemned in the Council's declaration on Christian-Jewish relations."[6]

Such recent statements as those by Carli and Saigh are no more than reiterations of attitudes which can unfortunately be found in some popular prayer books, and other Christian teaching media, still used throughout the world. For example, in the 1956 edition of Father J. F. Stedman's ≪ My Lenten Missal ≫, the following passage appears on page 269:

> In the Epistle [the Church] asks us to study the prayer of Azarias. His Jewish nation was suffering an exile of seventy years. . . . In these modern days, the Jews are still dispersed in every nation, in a condition worse than exile. They have been atoning these 1900 years for the greatest of all crimes, committed when an entire nation rejected, crucified, and shed the Blood of the Son of God.

In answer to Father Stedman and the Italian bishop, the Council's declaration states: "May, then, [catechists and preachers] see to it that . . . they do not teach anything that could give rise to hatred or contempt of Jews in the hearts of Christians. May they never present the Jewish people as one rejected, cursed, or guilty of deicide. All that happened to Christ in His passion cannot be attributed to the whole people then alive, much less to those of today."

And in answer to the Near Eastern prelate, the declaration states: "Moreover, this synod . . . deplores, indeed condemns, hatred and persecution of the Jews, whether they arose in former or in our own days."

Many more hopes, many more questions, come to mind. Wherever we go, questions are being asked. We would all like to know more about our mutual heritage, about the first centuries of Christian-Jewish conflict. Where are the culprits and where are the saints? More broadly, why do "a significant minority" of American Christians look upon the Jews as inferiors? What are the fictions and myths which create enmity between us, and how can we eradicate them? What are our real differences, and how can we bring our communities to understand and respect them?

Since the end of last November, our Catholic friends have been predicting smooth sailing for the declaration. I have not been quite so unreservedly sanguine. The ship, we hope and trust, will arrive at the port, but it will have to traverse some rough and stormy water en route. The Arabs, the Near Eastern patriarchs, and some bishops in Rome and other parts of the world will continue to exert pressure against the statement.

We are confident that, despite the unceasing pressure, the declaration in all probability will finally be adopted and promulgated by the Fourth Session of the Ecumenical Council. Some changes will be made; some changes have already been made in the text; but we trust that the spirit and substance of the document will be preserved.

In this atmosphere of anticipation of the final approval, it will be a tragedy of the first magnitude if we do not take the message of the declaration into our hearts and heads and hands, study the guidelines which it lays down so explicitly, and implement its teachings within the framework of our everyday lives. The declaration is not a tranquilizer for the Christian conscience or for Jewish fears. We have passed the stage of the ecumenism of the smile. The ecumenism of today is an invitation to action, the beginning of a new impetus toward greater Judeo-Christian understanding and cooperation. The document should be implemented, if it is not to become, tragically, simply a well-meant but ineffectual gesture of goodwill.

I ask these questions here, and raise these issues, which are intended to indicate some of the areas that need to be explored, because you are the touchstones of our society. Father John Courtney Murray recognized the sacerdotium and the studium, the church and the university, as the two major spiritual bulwarks in the life of the community, and stressed that institutions of higher learning have the duty to elaborate upon the public consensus in regard to "a high service of justice and the freedom of the people."7 The seminary also combines these two historically distinct spiritual forces, and becomes, in the words of Pope John, the "social conscience" of the nation. You are the religious teachers who will be speaking from pulpits, writing in newspapers and magazines, counseling congregations--in brief, you are the leaders. I have stressed the atmosphere of inquiry at the Council, because never before have leaders in both our communities been so free to investigate our relationships, both internal and external.

For centuries, we were blocked from open research and fruitful exchange by an atmosphere of hatred and suspicion which grew out of our fathers' fathers' bitter experiences and thus was taught to the sons. The last decade of years has done more than the last decade of centuries to change that atmosphere, to infuse it with understanding, cordial curiosity, and acceptance of responsibility for past ills. We are surrounded by fresh air and bright light; we need only breathe deeply and open our eyes.

(Footnotes follow on page 60.)

1 Condensation from English Clergy Review (September 1964) in Catholic Digest, March 1965.

2 Quoted in National Catholic Reporter, March 13, 1964.

3 Robert McAfee Brown, Observer in Rome: A Protestant Report on the Vatican Council (1964).

4 Quoted in New York Times, March 14, 1965.

5 Quoted in Boston Pilot, January 9, 1965.

6 George G. Higgins, "The Yardstick" (Syndicated column, NCWC News Service), January 25, 1965.

7 John Courtney Murray, We Hold These Truths (1961).

SEVEN

Reflections on the Ecumenical Council: a Catholic view

George G. Higgins

Director, Social Action Department
National Catholic Welfare Conference

Let me begin in a rather unusual way by quoting from a statement made by Pope Paul in a public lecture in Milan about two years before the Council opened. This statement was published in a pastoral letter and addressed itself to the subject of the impact of the Council on society and the world. In his pastoral message, the then Cardinal Montini took note of the historical fact that this Council, for the first time perhaps, would be free of political intervention or political interference. He said the world as such, that is, the civil or governmental order, has no direct relationship with this great forthcoming event, namely, the Council; that, unlike what had happened in the past, even up to the time of the Council of Trent, civil authority is entirely removed from the arena of ecclesiastical affairs. The progressive distinction and separation between church and state excluded any participation whatsoever

61

by civil society in the Council itself. It also excluded any interference by worldly powers and temporal interests in the course of the magnificent event, at once human and religious. Let us note it is in this fact of noninterference that modern secularism finds one of its expressions.

A few months later, while he was still in Milan as Archbishop of that See, Cardinal Montini returned to this theme by saying substantially the same thing. Civil society, he pointed out, and even the state itself, will completely ignore this episode in our contemporary history--the episode being, again, the Council. The distinction between church and state has reached its full expression even in those cases where there is no separation because the relations between the two societies have been defined by mutual agreement. The church and state remain two distinct societies. He then went on to say that this is an important development in the historical process and, applying it to the Council again, said that whatever may have been true in the past, civil societies will not now interfere with church negotiations. Not only will they not be represented officially, but they will stay out of the picture entirely.

Well, if you have ever had any question or doubt about the fact that Popes are infallible before or after they assume the throne, you can be sure this Pope was fallible before he came to Rome, because one of the central and unhappy facts about the declaration in relation to the Jews and other non-Christians is precisely the fact that the Arab Governments did become involved--not by sending representatives to the Vatican (which they were not entitled to do) but, so far as one can judge from the public record, by involving themselves in a number of other ways in a Council which tried desparately to stay on a purely religious level. The Council could not have done any more than it did to try to remove this problem from the political order. However, given the very complicated, delicate and explosive situation in the Middle East, the political element did become involved; and it played a substantial role, I am sure, in slowing down the final vote on the Schema or declaration.

I don't say that I can document the interference of the Arab Governments, although I suspect there are people who can and perhaps have already done so informally. However, I think it would be fair to say that there was a good bit of behind-the-scenes pressure from Arab spokesmen, trying to delay, if not to stop completely, any vote on the Jewish declaration.

I will not go into this in any more detail, but it is essential to bear this point in mind as one of the reasons why it took so long to get the issue off the ground and into conciliar debate. Whether we like it or not, there is a political element in the picture, but I think it must be ignored. I am sure the Council will ignore it when it completes the vote next fall. It would be most naive, however, to pretend to you that this issue doesn't exist or to pretend that the Council could just completely ignore it.

An issue which was closely related to this matter is the fact that even among certain unofficial circles in Israel itself, among Jewish spokesmen, there was a substantial amount of disagreement as to whether or not the Council should say anything about the Jews. This was not political in the strict sense, but it did have a bearing, I am sure, on the thinking of at least a few of the Fathers.

The same situation existed, to a much lesser extent, in this country. There was and is a minority group of Jewish spokesmen who, if I understand them and read them correctly, could not care less what the Council says or doesn't say on this question. As a matter of fact, they would like to have the Council mind its own business and to keep away from the Jewish question altogether. This, insofar as I know, is a factor in the situation in the United States, but it represents the point of view of a minority group among American Jews.

Many Jews, however, were not shocked about the revelation of the second draft--the one that hit the front page of the New York Herald Tribune, and on the following day the New York Times, so dramatically. Many Jews, as I say, were not shocked by this draft because they expected and wanted nothing of the Church except that it let the Jews alone, that it allow the Jews to live and to go to the Synagogue as they wished and to pursue their own way of life.

Let me also cite a very brief reference that came from an Israeli source in 1964, during the last session. This came from a newspaper under date of September 11th, and I quote here from the editorial: "We would do well to remember even in 1964 that we continue to exist thanks to generations of Jews who refuse to believe in the Christian Church as the harbinger of salvation. We do not live by what the Ecumenical Council says nor do we need the Church's Schema in one form or another to justify our existence and our Jewish entity." A similar editorial appeared in another Israeli paper about the same time.

Now, I am not suggesting that these are typical statements. How representative they are of the thinking in Israeli circles I would not know or would not pretend to know. However, they are sufficiently representative, I think, to have added one more fly to the ointment and to have given us reason to look at this thing in all of its complexity rather than to discuss it solely in terms of the theological problems which confront the Fathers when they are presented with the various and varying drafts of the declaration on the Jews.

The split in America, from what I know of it, seems to be much less representative than the point of view represented by Dr. Lichten and many others from the American Jewish organizations, but that need not detain us here.

We are fond of saying these days that theology must be historical. Theology does not exist in a vacuum. Neither does a Council. It exists in a very real world, and while I am not suggesting that the Council should give in to pressures or should take too much notice of disagreement in the Jewish Community, I think it would be naive and unrealistic to assume that both of these elements do not play their part. It is necessary, therefore, to keep both of these elements in the background if we want to understand the history of the Schema.

I know some Bishops, only a few to be sure, who took the position that if there were any disagreement in the Jewish Community, perhaps it would be better to say nothing. Of course, I did not agree with that point of view, but the idea was in the minds of some of the Bishops. I need hardly add that the other issue of Arab pressure was a much more serious problem and one which I am sure we will have with us up until the very moment that the final vote is taken next fall.

So much by way of a very general and roundabout introduction. I said earlier that I am not going to attempt to give you any scoop or inside story, because I know relatively little about the background of the Schema that most of you do not know. Many of you, perhaps, know even more about the Schema than I do, and therefore, I would not want to put my knowledge of it up against that of Joe Lichten or several others in the room.

If you want a reasonably good summary of the background of the Schema, I suppose you could do worse than go to the Commentary article of last January by F. E. Cartus, obviously a pen name. Needless to say, I don't subscribe to everything in this article, and of course, I am sorry that it was written under a pen name. I think we should have reached the stage by now, except possibly for certain individuals who have a vested interest in keeping their identity secret, to get away from this cloak-and-dagger routine and come out in the open with legitimate signatures to articles. If one knew for certain who Cartus is, then there are a number of statements in the article which he could assess much more objectively. Of course, I understand why Rynne did it in the first instance, and there may also be times in the future when it can be justified. However, there are certain historical and scholarly weaknesses to the approach which militate against it. In any event, if you want a summary statement concerning behind-the-scenes battle, you can find it in the Cartus article. I would only caution, as I have already done, that there is no way of telling, in the final analysis, whether all of Cartus' facts are completely accurate or whether some are based on pure hearsay or, at best, secondary sources.

I don't think there is any real need with this audience, which presumably has read more than the average audience would have read on the background and history of the draft, to go into details from the historical point of view. You know, of course, that there have been three public drafts and that no vote was taken on any of them until the last day of the last session. We often said in our little hideaway in Rome, in discussing this matter, that the experience at the end of each session could only be compared to the experience we had as kids of going to the Saturday-afternoon serial. The serial was designed to keep the audience on edge and keep them coming back for more. Well, I for one would like to come back, to keep going back and forth to Rome. However, I would certainly like to have this particular item decided once and for all. I could do without any additional suspense on this particular Schema.

There were, quite obviously, certain conservative groups within the Council which might have had theological misgivings about the deicide issue and other phases of the document, but I honestly think (and here I am perfectly willing to stand subject to correction) they were in a significant minority. This is something that the vote indicated at the end of the last session.

However, to summarize the history of the drafts very quickly, you may recall that the first draft was reasonably good. Then, between sessions, the draft was revised; and we come next to that day when the New York Herald Tribune, and subsequently the Times, broke the story in full text. The new draft eliminated any specific reference to the deicide charge and introduced, whether innocently or not (and I am inclined to think more innocently than some other critics believe), the so-called conversion issue. It was against that background--and the very heated controversy which those two issues aroused all over the world, but particularly in the United States--that the Fathers went back to the Council for their discussion of the draft.

The rest of the history is not too difficult to summarize because it has been so highly publicized. You may recall that the Council debated the second draft last September, from the 28th to the 30th of September. There were 35 speeches overwhelmingly in favor of a stronger draft. Only a handful of Bishops spoke against the draft, and even they spoke in terms of its being inopportune rather than contending that the draft itself was inadequate. Their argument, somewhat similar to the argument in Vatican I on Infallibility, was that it was not opportune at that time to introduce this matter for public discussion.

I am happy to report that the American Bishops did remarkably well on this issue. Indeed, I think it could be said that it was the vigorous insistence of the American spokesmen (and of others, but largely of the Americans) which made it absolutely certain that the second draft would have to be revised; that the deicide issue would have to be faced and the conversion issue would have to be clarified, if not completely eliminated. I am referring to speeches by Cardinals Meyer, Ritter and Cushing, and also a very good intervention by Archbishop O'Boyle, who directly addressed himself to the conversion issue. Bishop Leven and a number of others insisted quite vigorously that the second draft was unsatisfactory and quite specifically that the Council return to a strong statement on the deicide charge and that it clarify the conversion issue.

The document then went back, as is the normal process in the Council, to the appropriate Secretariat, which reviewed the oral interventions of the Bishops. Finally, on the last day of the Council, a new and revised draft was presented to the Fathers for the vote--which, as you know, was overwhelmingly in favor of the new text. The actual count of the vote, as I have it down here, was 1,651 in favor, 95 not in favor and 242 voting conditionally.

Now, I think it is most important to have clearly in mind just what this vote means. I have heard some of my Jewish friends who were not in Rome and are not familiar with the technicalities of the voting system in the Council say that these 242 conditional votes are rather dangerous because, conceivably, they would have enough influence to weaken the document. Actually, a qualified vote, according to the rules of the Council, is an affirmative vote. So, there were really only 95 negative votes. Of course, no one knows what refinement the 242 votes called for. I am not on that Commission and have not seen a breakdown of the votes, but I think it would be a fair and reasonable guess to say that many of them are asking for more than is contained in the present draft, for clarifications which would strengthen it. In any event, they are conditional votes--not negative votes.

The Commission met some two or three weeks ago. I am not privy to what went on in the confidential sessions of the Commission, but I have talked to a number of people who did take part in the meetings. They have all assured me that the document is in good shape. It is quite possible that changes have been made in the wording of the draft, but being an optimist, I would assume, on the basis of what these men have told me, that these changes were not substantial and that, in any event, they did not weaken the text.

The only source (in addition to the oral assurances I have received from several men who participated in the meetings of the Commission) that I have to go on is one you have all seen, namely, the story in the New York Times. This left me with the impression that the Schema is in good shape.

We are all mature and sophisticated people. Therefore, we can assume that this decrease in public conflict doesn't mean there will be no pressure between now and the vote next fall. Quite obviously, there will be. In fact, there will be continuous pressure from the Arab world. There will be the kind of pressure that Dr. Lichten referred to when he quoted Bishop Carli's statement as presented in that Italian clerical magazine. I have never seen that article, but if it is typical of the magazine's approach, then I don't think I am going to subscribe.

Bishop Carli, on the other hand, did something I think quite admirable. He has been accused, perhaps excessively, by his critics in the Council, of working behind the scenes. However, he did not work behind the scenes this time at all; he came right out and stated his theological position, with which I happen to disagree and with which I am sure the Council is going to disagree. This is the kind of pressure I regret, but only in the sense that the man is holding to something I think is untenable. However, I think it is a legitimate way of making his views known on a matter before the Council.

Now, with regard to my own position on the Schema. It is the same as that of Dr. Lichten and others from the various Jewish groups with whom I have worked in Rome: the promulgation by the Council of a stronger document than the one the Fathers voted on last fall is a matter of utmost importance. If the Council fails on this issue, it will have made a tragic mistake, but I myself don't think it will fail. I expect a good text to come out, with an overwhelming vote, sometime in the course of the fourth and final session of the Council.

The importance of this vote is beyond question. It may be of some importance, however, to add a word of caution, which others have already done in the course of our few days here. Dr. Lichten himself did this yesterday.

My first word of caution is that it would be foolish, if not naive, to expect that this decree, if it is adopted, will change the course of history in a few short years. This is a caution which it would be wise for us to keep in mind in considering not only this issue but a number of other issues before the Council. If Pope John made any major mistake in his handling of the Council (and I say this very respectfully), it was, I think, in unwittingly building up overly optimistic expectations--expectations not only of people outside the Church but of Catholics themselves.

You can see this very clearly, of course, in the case of Schema 13 on the Church and the modern world. I am absolutely certain that many Catholics--and, by the same token, I presume, even more non-Catholics--are going to be seriously disappointed in Schema 13 because they are expecting something from the Schema which, in my personal opinion, the Schema should not be expected to give them. I would go even further and say that I would not want the Schema to attempt to give them absolute Catholic answers to some of the most vexing problems facing the modern world. What I would suggest, in broad terms, is that we be realistic enough to approach any of the decrees of the Council with a certain historical perspective and to realize that the promulgation of an important decree, whether on the subject of Jewish-Christian relations or on the nature of the Church, on ecumenism or whatever, is only the beginning and not the end of the process. This realistic approach puts us in a better position to begin to do things that might have been harder to do without such a document.

Secondly, may I direct a very frank word of caution to my Jewish friends in the audience. I have said this before to many of you privately and would like to say it publicly here today. I think the cause (and here again I am subject to correction by my Catholic conferees) of Christian-Jewish relations will be hindered, rather than helped, if the impression is created that all or almost all Christians, because of their catechetical training and religious instruction, have a built-in tendency to accept the deicide charge. I have discussed this matter quite openly with Rabbi Tannenbaum in public meetings.

I would also say to you one other thing--that if I were a Bishop and if I thought that by voting for this Schema I would thereby be saying that all Christians or all Catholics have, up until now, accepted the deicide charge because of their religious training, I would vote against the Schema. I don't think that people should be forced by the inevitable tensions created around this issue to vote for something which would imply something that they do not accept.

I can only say honestly that I cannot think of anything for which I would have been punished more severely, in my home as a boy, than if I had suggested, even remotely or indirectly, that I thought the Jews were Christ-killers. Therefore, I don't want to be responsible for the deicide charge, and there are many other Christians who do not want to be responsible either.

What I am suggesting, therefore, is that we do not attribute all anti-Semitism to theological presuppositions or misunderstandings. I do not deny the crucial importance of the theological and Biblical approach to this problem. Psychologically speaking, I can only say, for whatever it is worth, that those in the Jewish Community most interested in promoting a better understanding between the two faiths, Jewish and Christian, will hurt rather than help the cause if they exaggerate the extent of the participation of Christians in the terrible deicide charge or in the perpetuation of this terrible charge.

One other caution on a matter which has already been discussed, in other contexts, by several of the speakers. The dialogue between Jews and Christians simply must be a two-way street. There simply has to be a willingness on the part of both groups to be self-critical. I refer to this again because, a day or two before I left Washington to come to Chicago, a very good friend of mine in the Jewish Community in Washington made a speech on the school question which many of you have seen quoted in the press. I think I understand why there is so much intense feeling among Jews on the constitutional aspects of this question, and to a large extent I agree with them. It is embedded deeply in their history, and I don't think that any Christian, without a superhuman effort, can really put himself in the position of the Jew when he comes to confront this issue.

Therefore, I am not raising the question to talk about the constitutional aspects, nor am I suggesting for a moment, as some Christians have mistakenly done, that the Jews should keep quiet on this issue for fear of offending Christian sensitivities. What I am suggesting is that there is a real danger, in my mind, at least, that the constitutional issue will be rationalized as a cover for a certain amount of anti-Catholicism.

This, I think, became clear in a very serious way in the answer given to this friend of mine by another Jewish spokesman who was defending the government's position on the educational aspects of the poverty program. With the best of goodwill and in a way which I think I can understand, this spokesman, in trying to convince his audience that they ought to go along with the educational aspects of the poverty bill, said, "Remember, keep in mind that the Catholic Church after Vatican II is not the same Church as it was before." This, it seems to me, raises a religious issue relative to what has previously been called a constitutional issue, and it is this kind of issue which I think must be sifted out of the legitimate concern of the Jewish Community about the separation of church and state in the educational field. The present state of Catholicism has nothing to do with the American constitution.

There are other issues of this kind which I think must be discussed with the greatest of frankness, or otherwise the dialogue will become, in my judgment, meaningless and a waste of time. My life at this stage is much too short to engage in a dialogue in which frankness is not the order of the day. Indeed, I cannot think of any worse insult that a Catholic priest could give a Protestant or Jewish friend than to flatter him or agree with him when he actually did not agree with him. Flattery, I think, is the most despicable type of insult, because it assumes that the man you are dialoguing with is incapable of arguing matters out in the open without taking offense.

Finally, I have already said that I think that the decree or declaration is not going to work any wonders overnight. I do think, however, that it will go a long, long way toward making it possible to move ahead at many levels of thought and activity in the future. It will, furthermore, if I may hazard a guess, make this kind of dialogue so popular that even those of us whose profession requires them to get out to meetings constantly will finally reach the point where they will be dictating the standard letters--"Because of a previous commitment, I regret . . ." There will be so many meetings of this type, I am sure, that many of us will find it difficult to give them the time they require.

One final word about the Council in general. I think it would be a mistake to concentrate so exclusively on the Jewish declaration as to ignore the broader work of the Council which, in many ways, may have more to do with the solution of the problem we have been discussing than the specific Schema on Christian-Jewish relations.

That is true in so many areas. Let me cite but one from my own experience in the Council. There is to be a vote next fall on a Schema on the lay apostolate. I am convinced it will be much less important for the lay apostolate than the Schema on the Church passed last year. Of course, it is a necessary adjunct to the Schema on the Church, but the essential doctrine has already been stated in the latter document.

I would suggest, by the same token, that even though there is no explicit discussion of the Jewish question in the Schema on the Church, in the long run, this Schema will probably do more to solve the problems we are worrying about here than even the specific Schema or declaration on the Jews. The reason for this has already been suggested by many of the theologians and Biblical professors here today: only with a better understanding of the Church, on the part of the Church itself, will the Church be able to do many of the things in specific areas that it must do if it is going to be faithful to its witness.

In that same context, it is perfectly obvious, I think, and hardly needs to be emphasized, that the Schema or declaration on religious liberty will in many ways have a direct bearing on the question we are talking about here today. Now, of course, Jerry Brauer would like me to tell you where the Schema on religious liberty is. Unlike the declaration on the Jews, it was not voted on last time. However, I have been assured that the document is in good shape, that it has not been weakened and will come up for a vote in the fall. When it does, it is a foregone conclusion it will be adopted by an overwhelming vote.

The argument over the Schema, as you know better than I do, was a complicated one. There were some people who did not want a declaration or Schema on religious liberty--period. Again, however, I think they are in a very small minority. The important argument, the one that is to be given the most serious consideration, is the one among the theologians themselves as to how to approach the subject theologically, how to state the premises. It was, I think, quite predictable that Father John Courtney Murray's approach would not go unchallenged by the French theologians and others who come from the French tradition.

What happened at the meeting a few weeks ago, as I understand it, is that they reached some sort of reasonable compromise between various points of view. This is the stage at which the argument is today. Again, there will be opposition to the declaration in the fall but, I think, much less perhaps than we feared two or three weeks ago. Finally, I am confident that it will be adopted by an overwhelming vote at the final session of the Council.

EIGHT

The World Council of Churches and Judaism

Amos N. Wilder

Hollis Professor of Divinity, Emeritus
Harvard Divinity School

There are two contexts today in which Jewish-Christian relations have been or can be most deeply explored: on the one hand
as Christians have honestly faced what they can learn about themselves from the Hitler period; on the other hand in the ecumenical
movement. The first context explains the new breakthrough that
has occurred in some continental theology and that found its
clearest expression in the Berlin Kirchentag in 1961. The second
context, the ecumenical, indebted to the first, is equally prom-
ising.

In comparison with these, two older contexts suffer under some
limitations: the missionary tradition, and the denominational approach. As far as the missionary movement is concerned, granted
its prodigious ministries in past and present and its changing
character, there is question whether it has been able to recognize

fully the unique significance of the Jewish community and the corollaries for interfaith relations at this point. One can raise such question even with regard to the 1963 meeting in Mexico City of the World Council's Commission on World Mission and Evangelism. It is true that the merging of the International Missionary Council with the World Council of Churches at New Delhi in 1961 brought the perspectives of the missionary movement more fully into the ecumenical movement, an enrichment of both. By the limitations of the denominational approach I mean that no one Christian body or confession can deal alone with so fundamental a topic, as appears even in the case of the Vatican Council or the World Lutheran Convention at its meeting on this topic in Denmark in 1963.

One justification for having a statement on the World Council and Judaism in our present meeting is that the Council has become something of a forum for the chief issues of the churches today. While it does not claim to speak for the member churches, the various views and activities of these bodies find some confrontation in its assemblies and consultations. The WCC combines the special interest in our topic represented by the International Missionary Council and the vigorous theological concern which it is bringing to many topics, especially ecclesiological. It is also today in the process of responding to the requests made to it on various occasions to formulate guidance to its member churches with regard to all that has to do with the relations of the Church and the Jewish people. I believe that the importance of this guidance will lie in the fact that it will rest on shared ecumenical study, that it will benefit from the deep reappraisal into which all Christians must have been shocked by the mass persecutions of the recent period, and that it will also benefit by the new stage which has been reached in biblical and biblical-theological studies.

But the special importance of an ecumenical approach to our topic can be brought out in another way. If we retrace the history of sectarianism and disunity back behind the great divisions of the Church we do not stop with the Reformation or the earlier breach between Rome and the East. We come finally to the breach between Christian and Jew, and in a real sense this belongs in the same series if we understand aright the meaning of election and the People of God. But this is only to say that it is from within the ecumenical movement that the real inwardness of the separation of Jew and Christian can be grasped. Any one confession or church deals with this fateful cleavage, once removed at least from actuality, and is handicapped by its own family history. It is only when together the churches make a deeply humble and contrite effort toward unity that Christianity as a whole can overcome that history which sealed the original separation from the synagogue. For however inevitable we may see that separation to have been, there have been from the beginning adventitious features which we should get behind.

This ecumenical aspect of our question was well stated in a declaration on "Israel and the Church" by the Dutch Reformed Church in 1959. After calling upon the faithful to recognize that the Church is the younger sister of Israel in the providential witness to God, and should give a full hearing to the synagogue in true dialogue, the statement continues:

> We can indeed go a step farther and consider our relation to Israel in an ecumenical light, since we regard the cleavage between Church and Israel as the first schism within the one body of the congregation of God. Israel was the cradle of the oecumene. This conception is so closely linked with the People of Israel, that an ecumenical movement cuts itself off from its own origin if it does not concern itself with its relation to this People. For apart from Israel the Church cannot experience in full measure its own ecumenical character.[1]

We may also cite here a statement of Prof. Karl Kupisch who is speaking of the shock of Auschwitz, etc., in calling forth a sharp reappraisal of existing views in the Church with regard to the Jews. But this, he continues,

> . . . cannot possibly be the affair of any one single Church. Just as the mass-murder of Jews in Europe aroused the whole of world-Jewry, so the whole of Christendom is involved in the theological consequences to be drawn from the event. All the more it should be self-evident that all questions which touch the life of the Church are to be seen as ecumenical.[2]

It is one thing for our churches to rebuke prejudice and error, to acknowledge guilt and complicity in public hysteria, to condemn crass forms of propaganda and proselytism, and to invite to honest dialogue. All this can be done at a relatively superficial level, and without opening up radically the securities of our various ecclesiastic and confessional traditions. But in our costly wrestling for unity, when Christians divided from each other for centuries must seek the deepest meaning of the Gospel and the total purpose of God in the light of both covenants, we find ourselves at a point in our relation to Israel like that in the earliest fluid period of Christian origins. Here the unfolding meaning of God's work in the midst of his People was still a dynamic open question. No doubt those Jews who believed in the Gospel saw in Christ the Amen and the fulfillment of all the promises of God, as Christians do today. But Israel as a whole in faithfulness to God's covenant as they understood it could not agree, and they have continued in their faithfulness to this day. The full meaning of God's work in that drama and the full meaning of Christ himself will not be known until the "end," and that meaning will include and surpass the witness of both Israel and the Church. In this sense the meaning of God's work in the Gospel remains an open question to this day, and Israel's witness to the meaning of election and covenant and to the understanding of its Scriptures remains essential.

We cannot here review in detail the earlier stages of ecumenical concern with the Jews. The year 1930 saw the foundation, under the International Missionary Council, of the Committee on the Christian Approach to the Jews. Already numerous churches and societies devoted to the mission to Jews had held large meetings. It is interesting to sample the addresses given at the Atlantic City Conference in 1931 of the North American Section of the International Committee on the Christian Approach to the Jews. Speakers included John R. Mott, Conrad Hoffmann, Basil Mathews, Samuel Swemer, Julius Richter and others. The limitations of independent missions are pointed out. They had arisen in the ghetto situation which was passing in this country. They were often headed by converted Jews, and they were open to the charge of using questionable incentives. Hoffmann, who headed the Committee for a long period, urged that work among the Jews should be carried out as part of regular parish work, that special training should be given to those engaged in this field, and that Judaism should be better known. The Jews should be taught to appreciate their own heritage, said Basil Mathews, and the synagogue should be seen as an ally against the demoralization of culture. But there is very little theological depth. To those who objected to Jewish missions, the International Missionary Council replied:

> It is true . . . that Christianity as well as Mohammedanism, has its roots in Judaism but it is only one of these three religions that recognizes Jesus of Nazareth as Christ. Judaism is as much without Christ as Mohammedanism and

Hinduism, Buddhism and Confusionism. Either all people need Christ or none.[3]

At the First Assembly of the WCC at Amsterdam in 1948 a statement titled "The Christian Approach to the Jews" was commended to the churches for serious consideration and action. This statement opens with an evocation of the very recent deportations from Holland and the extermination of millions of Jews. The place of Israel in God's design is stated. Anti-Semitism is condemned and the guilt of the churches is acknowledged. The Christian witness to the Jewish people is urged, but "as a normal part of parish work" rather than by special agencies, and with avoidance of "all unworthy pressures." The WCC and the International Missionary Council are called upon to recognize the need of more detailed studies as to contemporary factors, but theological and biblical studies are not here mentioned.[4]

It should be noted that in the early forties and after the war vigorous concern for the situation of the Jews under the Hitler program and in the aftermath of the war was voiced by Christian bodies acting in concert. There were also practical activities for relief and resettlement. The « News Sheet » of the International Committee on the Christian Approach to the Jews for those years makes extremely interesting reading today. Here was one Christian organization which served as a clearinghouse and an information center with respect to every aspect of the changing situation of the Jews, and which laid their needs upon the conscience both of churchmen and statesmen.[5]

We should also recall the Second Assembly of the WCC in Evanston. In the report presented to it by the Advisory Committee on the main theme, Christ, the Hope of the World, there were references to the ultimate place of Israel in God's promises in Christ. Objections were made on the one hand by representatives of the churches in the Near East on the ground that mention of Israel would make the task of these churches more difficult. It will also be remembered that a well-known American lay delegate objected that the tenor of these references was not "the way to start a mission to the Jews"; they would, moreover, "jeopardize relations of members of the Assembly with their Jewish friends." The Assembly voted to eliminate the references to Israel by a vote of 195 to 150. In the sequel, however, a statement presented by Professor Sittler and signed by 24 delegates was received for record. This widely influential statement speaks of the grievous guilt of Christian people toward the Jews throughout the history of the Church; notes that "we are grafted into the old tree of Israel (Romans 11:24), so that the people of the New Covenant cannot be separated from the people of the Old Covenant"; and holds that "the Church cannot rest until the title of Christ is recognized by His own people according to the flesh."

The Evanston Assembly passed a resolution calling upon the Central Committee of the WCC to promote the study of these matters. This led to what still remains the most careful statement for the WCC, that of the Bossey Consultation in September 1956. The International Missionary Council shared in the planning. The statement evokes all the reasons for which the Church should approach the Jews with humility and with a recognition of Israel's unique role in the purpose of God. This leads to a strong emphasis on dialogue as the proper form of confrontation. "We shall not single out the Jewish people for particular attention in evangelism, where that would only emphasize the separation which we seek to overcome." With respect to the State of Israel, it is stated that "we cannot say a plain yes." Nor can we say a plain no, "because the Church does not stand for a vague cosmopolitanism." Moreover, "Judaism has an abiding message for the Church in its stress on the revelation through the Law and the Prophets, that God is Lord over every realm of life, material as well as spiritual."

At the Third Assembly at New Delhi in 1961 a short statement was approved. It confined itself to reinforcing the rebuke of anti-Semitism voted at the First Assembly. Of special significance is the following:

> In Christian teaching the historic events which led to the Crucifixion should not be so presented as to fasten upon the Jewish people of today responsibilities which belong to our corporate humanity and not to one race or community. Jews were the first to accept Jesus and Jews are not the only ones who do not yet recognize him.

Throughout the recent period there have been recurrent requests made to the WCC that more fundamental study should be given to the whole subject. This was true, for example, of the Fourth World Conference on Faith and Order, meeting in Montreal in 1963. The report of Section I on "Christ and the Church" has the following note:

> The question of God's purpose in the Old Covenant and the New was raised. . .; it emerged also in our discussions, but in a context where extended discussion was impossible. The

77

place of Israel requires careful study, and we strongly recommend that the subject be referred to a commission.

Even more recent was the meeting in Mexico City in December 1963 of the Commission on World Mission and Evangelism of the WCC. The changing conception of Christian missions as a whole was registered here in the emphasis on dialogue, and recognition was made of the wide disparity of attitudes among those approached. The paragraph regarding Israel includes the following:

> As we believe that Christ is both the fulfilment of the covenant and the light of the world, we must be willing to listen to what the Jew has to say to us in his interpretation of the covenant, but also to bear unmistakable witness to Christ as the Way, the Truth, and the Life, as we would to the followers of any other faith than our own.

The new phase of the concern of the WCC with our topic is to be identified with the Consultation on Israel and the Church which met in Geneva, September 21 to 26, 1964. It was called together jointly by the Commission on Faith and Order and the Committee on the Church and the Jewish People, represented by Lukas Vischer and Anker Gjerding respectively, and was chaired by Erich Dinkler of the University of Heidelberg. In the invitation to participants Dr. Vischer wrote:

> You know that several ecumenical conferences have touched upon the question of the significance of the people of Israel, but that so far no agreement has been reached. On the contrary, the differences were so great that it seemed impossible to overcome them. However, during the last few years many member churches of the World Council have renewed discussion of this question and we therefore think it advisable to take it up again on an ecumenical level. It is no mere coincidence that two of the Theological Commissions which had prepared the reports for the World Conference in Montreal independently stressed the importance of this subject for the ecumenical discussion. They came to this conclusion because they recognized that in dealing with this question other ecclesiological problems too might appear in a new light.

It was anticipated that a draft statement would be drawn up by the Consultation which would then be submitted to the member churches for comment, after which an enlarged group would work out a more definitive statement. Participants in the Constitution were asked to deal with the problem under the following three points of view:

a) How is the continuous existence of Israel after Christ to be interpreted?

b) What does the vis-à-vis of the Church and Israel mean for the self-understanding of the Church?

c) Can we make any recommendations to the member churches of the WCC for the living together of the Church and Israel?

Members of the Consultation who actually attended, apart from those already mentioned and myself, were as follows: from the WCC and the Ecumenical Institute, M. B. H. Handspicker, H. H. Wold; from Switzerland, J.-L. Leuba; from England, P. R. Ackroyd, E. W. Heaton, H. Montefiore; from Germany, K. Kupisch; from Denmark, J. M. Aagaard; from the Netherlands, E. Flesseman-Van Leer. Before the meeting a compilation of the most significant statements on the question by ecumenical meetings and by member churches was given to the participants. In the opening sessions statements were made by several members with regard to Jewish-Christian relationships and the state of theological discussion in various countries.[6]

It will be noted that the participation of Professor Kupisch brought into the discussion the concerns of one of those who had taken an active part in the notable Section 6 on the Jews at the Berlin Kirchentag in 1961 and its later activities. Professor Aagaard of Aarhus had participated actively in the 1964 meeting on the Church and the Jews of the World Lutheran Federation in Denmark. Dr. Vischer, as a delegate-observer at the Vatican Council, at this very time occupied with our topic, brought another important contact into our exploration. It was regrettable that our Orthodox member was able to participate only briefly.

The draft statement drawn up by the Consultation is provisional in character and is looked upon as a working paper. It is to be circulated to interested individuals and study groups with a view to comments and reactions.[7] Following another Consultation to be held in 1966, the text will be revised and even entirely recast.

The resulting statement will then be submitted to the Faith and Order Commission at its meeting in 1967.

The present report, however, already points toward the form of the eventual statement to be adopted by the WCC. One basic feature, no doubt, will be an insistence on the new light shed on the whole topic by recent biblical-theological understanding of Scripture. The issues as to continuity and discontinuity of the Old and the New Covenants and the profound solidarity of Church and Israel are being better understood. Our better grasp of the meaning of election, covenant and the faithfulness of God rule out widespread views of the rejection of unbelieving Israel and divine punishment of that people. Christians must awaken to the fact that subtle forms of crypto-Marcionism have infected the outlook of the Church and its theology and have failed to do justice to the fundamental significance of the Old Testament and to the fact that the synagogue shares with the Church in witness to the living God of the covenants and his faithfulness. This recognition of the uniqueness of the Jewish people also imposes a radical difference in the way in which Christians witness their faith to the Jews. Some will understand the doctrine of election in such a way--i.e., that the Jews are today a part of the sundered People of God--that any form of mission will be excluded. Others will in any case be painfully conscious of what the name of Christ must mean in the light of the recent holocaust, and witness will take the form either of silent deeds of justice and goodness or of dialogue without ulterior motives. Others will so state it as to say that witness is in the nature of the case mandatory for the Christian, but that in our relations with the Jews our witness will be illumined by theirs. An eventual document of the WCC will no doubt also contain counsel to the churches with regard to prevailing misunderstandings that occasion prejudice, especially misunderstandings of the Gospels.

It should be emphasized that the concern of the WCC goes beyond the topic of Jewish-Christian relations to that of a truer understanding of the Church and the Gospel. There is scarcely any disputed area in recent ecumenical encounter which is not illuminated by our subject. The meaning of historical revelation as Israel and the Old Testament understand it challenges many forms of Christian subjectivism and spirituality. The covenant-law of Israel calling for the sanctification of daily life in this world challenges a great deal of Christian other-worldliness. That God elects and acts through an empirical people should have more to say to us about the nature of the Church and about how God deals with the nations. Dialogue with the synagogue, finally, makes it impossible for the Church to avoid a constant reassessment of its understanding of Christ and of the Trinity.

The present attention of the WCC to the subject is also illustrated by its Graduate School of Ecumenical Studies at the Ecumenical Institute at Bossey. For each academic year a main theme is chosen. In the 13th Session for 1964-65 the theme has been The Elect People of God in the Service of the World. This formulation of the topic suggests the common origin of Israel and the Church within the historical revelation of God and their common vocation of the service of the world. About fifty students from eighteen countries and ten confessions were enrolled. An excellent library for the topic has been available, and much of the work has been done in small groups.

The first term, in which I took part, was given to biblical and historical studies. An historical introduction was provided by Prof. G. D. Kilpatrick of Oxford and by a Jewish lecturer, Johanan Bloch of Berlin. Study of the Old Testament was led by Prof. Martin-Achard of Geneva; of the New, by Prof. Wilhelm Vischer and myself. Lectures on the life and liturgy of the synagogue were given by the Grand Rabbi of Geneva, Alexandre Safran. In the group discussions we had the services of different members of the Bossey staff and WCC leaders: Wolf, Nissiotis, Weber, Verghese, Parmat, Gjerding. In our discussions with our Jewish colleagues I cannot well convey the moving experience that was ours in the most searching dialogue and affectionate mutual appreciation.

In its second term the Graduate School turned to contemporary issues, such as anti-Semitism today and the State of Israel. Further leaders have included Professors Gollwitzer (Berlin), Berkhof (Leiden), Werblowsky and Chouraqui (Jerusalem).

The outcome of this program at the Ecumenical Institute will certainly feed back into all further work of the WCC. Participating students will take back their own experience into many parts of the Christian world. The methods employed, which made much of close biblical exegesis in small groups as well as of interfaith meeting at a profound level, should commend themselves for wider practice. It will be recalled that a year or more ago at Mexico City plans were endorsed for an ecumenical study center in Israel, as well as for a Christian-Muslim study center in Nigeria. In connection with the former Bishop Newbigin stated that "better facilities are needed to bring about a true encounter between the gospel and Israel and to rethink the character of Christian witness to the Jewish people and to improve Jewish-Christian relationships." One may hope that any such center in Jerusalem may focus first of all as at Bossey upon a study by the churches of their own self-understanding with the help of Jewish participants.

81

Let me make the following observations in conclusion.

(1) There will continue to be widely different views among the member churches of the World Council. Any statement made will presumably include divergent views. Because of the profound and tragic character of Christian disunity the quest for agreement on this topic also will be a costly one. The most important factors in disagreement are the varying views of Scripture and its inter-pretation. The WCC Study Department is just embarking upon a series of hermeneutical studies by regional groups. One special factor in disagreement is the situation of member churches in the Middle East.

(2) While the WCC will be deeply concerned about contemporary applications of its findings, its primary contribution will have to do with the theological bases of such matters. And while the WCC will seek to further all aspects of Jewish-Christian relations, its primary interest will be in an encounter between Jews and Christians deeply committed to their respective revelations, covenants and ethical obligations. It is only at this level that the Christian, for his part, can hope to open up significantly the deeper meaning of the Church and the conditions of unity.

(3) The point of greatest promise for our mutual relations lies in our attack, not only upon overt prejudice, but upon the causes of latent anti-Semitism. Because of historical factors our various churches have a subtle built-in sense of justification and spiritual security which lames the Christian life and vitiates our relation with the synagogue. In one way or another the very real blessings of faith are objectified into a secure possession. As against the Jew the Christian is deeply persuaded that he already reigns. He forgets Paul's warning: "What hast thou that thou hast not received?" This misunderstanding goes back to a loss of that inward surprised sense of undeserved election and what it meant in the New Testament: that al was in God's hand and not in ours. I say that there is promise at this point today, because we are learning that there is only one Elect Peopl of God, though a cleavage was introduced into it in the divine providen in the period we know. We should learn not to speak of the Church as t "new" Israel or the "true" Israel or the "spiritual" Israel. It is rather to be understood, in Berkhof's phrase, as the "eschatological, univers izing shape of Israel."

(4) The most difficult aspect of this built-in security and self-justification of the churches is their understanding of Christ. No doubt there is an impassable gulf here between Jews and Christians so far as any human wisdom reaches. But there are unnecessary exasperations of this disagreement, what one can call secularizations

of the doctrines, which both rebuff the Jew and others and distort the Gospel. It is at this point that the new critical biblical theology becomes so important, and WCC consultations will be entirely open to its findings. We must go behind the New Testament Christology in two senses: behind the formulas to their dynamic meaning in the Jewish eschatological context; and back before them into that period in which the earliest Christian witness--and still an intra-Jewish witness--was in the making. There, as I have said earlier, we rejoin that deeper fluid situation where the meaning of God's work in the midst of his People was not as yet a closed matter--and in a sense it is never closed. This is where we seek to stand today that we may together learn more of the depth of the riches both of the wisdom and knowledge of God.

As children of Adam, all of us, there is only one temptation from the beginning, a temptation that underlies all others: not to think largely enough about the charity of God. We circumscribe the magnanimity of God. And this may sometimes be the temptation of the synagogue in its thinking about the Church. What was it that drove the early Christian witnesses out into the no-man's-land from the confines of the Law? And it is certainly a temptation of the Church in its thinking about the synagogue. We, all of us, need to think largely about the charity and the wisdom and the knowledge of God. In the measure that the divine magnanimity is grasped, the underlying oneness of the People of God manifests itself, whether between church and church, or between Israel and Church.

1 Cited in Der Ungekuendigte Bund (Eds., D. Goldschmidt and H.-J. Kraus). Stuttgart, 1962, p. 281. Cf. Skydsgaard, The Lutheran Quarterly, October 1963, p. 350.

2 "Nach Auschwitz: Fragen an die Weltchristenheit." WCC Division of Studies, FO/64:50 (b), August 1964. The author is a professor in the Kirchliche Hochschule in West Berlin.

3 Göte Hedenquist, "Twenty-five Years of the International Missionary Council's Committee on the Christian Approach to the Jews." Uppsala, 1957, p. 5.

4 In the light of this request a Committee was set up by the WCC and the outcome was a volume of papers published in 1954, edited by Göte Hedenquist, The Church and the Jewish People. This volume has the merit of including papers by two Jewish writers, H. J. Schoeps and Leo Baeck. Most of the papers by Christian con-tributors present the obligation of Christian witness to the Jews

in rather conventional terms. Even the most important theological discussion, that of K. H. Rengstorf, would appear infelicitous as a basis for dialogue.

5 See especially the Recommendations of the International Committee on the Christian Approach to the Jews, as approved by the Ad Interim Committee of the International Missionary Council, Geneva, February 1946. This calls for a survey of world Jewry, for study of Zionism and the future of Palestine, and of the "underlying factor of growing anti-Semitism," for continued ministry to refugees of Jewish origin, especially the Hebrew Christians, for attention to the "parish approach" in relation to the Jews. One interesting feature of the statement is the link made between the fact of anti-Semitism and the obligation of the Christian mission to the Jews. "Nothing less than the inclusion of the Jews in the evangelistic programme of the Christian Church on equal terms with other races and religions can fulfill our Christian duty to this persecuted people." News Sheet of the International Committee on the Christian Approach to the Jews, vol. XVI, no. 1 (January-March, 1946), p. 6.

6 Papers were also distributed and discussed by Prof. P. R. Ackroyd, "The Church and Israel: The Biblical Evidence"; Prof. K. Kupisch, "Theses for Discussion"; Prof. J.-L. Leuba, "Christ, Israel and the Church: A Systematic Study."

7 Those interested may secure the present report (FO/65:7) from the WCC Division of Studies. It should be borne in mind, however, that this working paper is not an official document of the WCC and must not be quoted or used as such. Those interested in securing the compilation of statements concerning the relationship between the Jewish people and the Church produced by World Council meetings may obtain it (in mimeographed form, at the price of Sw Fr 7) from the Publications Office of the WCC.

NINE

Panel talk on curriculum:
Judaism and Christian biblical studies

J. Coert Rylaarsdam
Professor of Old Testament
The Divinity School, University of Chicago

Let me begin by saying that over the years I have had a great many students in my courses in the Divinity School who were representatives of the Jewish faith. Therefore, I have become increasingly sensitive to the fact that there are two perspectives at work in my classroom. One becomes increasingly sensitive to the fact that Jews read the Bible in a different way than do the Christian students. That is, that part of the Bible which they share with Christians is read differently. However, I have found that learning to read it their way as well as reading it my way is a very fruitful experience, one which leads to all kinds of important issues related to Jewish-Christian biblical scholarship.

What I want to emphasize is that in my classes I have increasingly evaluated Judaism not in terms of how we ought to respect it, how we ought to be tolerant of it, or how we ought to recognize its social and human equality with the Christian tradition--all of which are very significant dimensions. But, more and more, I have been raising the question of whether there are not certain dimensions of Jewish witness without which our whole society and our common life would be impoverished.

What has impressed me most in my academic years in the University is that one finds in the Bible, notably in the Old Testament, and in the Jewish tradition a faith that leads to a preoccupation with this life, with the importance and significance of time, space, and matter--not simply an importance of these in the past, culminating in the Incarnation, but an importance of these that is perennial from the Jewish point of view. We call this stance "biblical realism." Such a faith is eminently pre-occupied with time, space, and matter as media of divine disclosure.

Now if there is anything that is pervasively characteristic of Western Civilization, it is that it has developed a perennial concern for technological know-how. It is a worldly civilization that thinks it is important to deal with the processes and riches of time, space, and matter, with the world of history and humanity. We do this, for the most part, simply on the human level. This is the way in which man can attain a certain ascendency over the world of nature. However, if you go back to the Bible, to the first chapter of Genesis, God states, "Let us make man in our own image and let him have dominion." The realization of man's potential for the manipulation of and dominion over nature is written into the Bible. The idea is that since God is working in, through, and by means of these processes, our working in, through, and by means of these processes puts us into a close connection with reality, with God.

We do not find reality in the Bible of the Jew by going out of the world, as some have mistakenly supposed. We find it by moving into the world ever more intensely. This, I think, is the inspiration for Western Civilization's preoccupation with the technological dimension of human life, with its concern to make this world livable. As a result of this positive attitude toward the world of time and space, the world we use is sacred and our use of it (dedicated to the will of Him who made it) is a sacred use. This idea has almost been completely lost in many Christian circles. The doctrine of Creation is a lost article of the Creed, certainly in large sections of Protestant Christianity. Therefore, it is this sense of the immanent presence of God in the Community of Israel that, I believe, raises the question of the positive role

86

of the Judaic faith and its continuing witness in our society today.

Furthermore, on the moral and ethical level, I find something absolutely indispensable in Judaism. Rabbi Heschel said on one occasion: "Do you really want to live in a world without Jews?" I, for one, would not like to live in the United States without Jews because, in a very profound sense, I as a Christian have to say that socially and ethically speaking, the Jew is the salt of this society, the conscience, the social, moral, ethical leaven of the nation. That is, in many ways the Jew is more acutely alive in awareness than is the Christian.

Do not misunderstand me. I am not saying that Christians are completely negligent in exercising a decisive and effective moral mission. I am not beating my breast about the lack of initiative for social reform on the part of Christians. There is, from time to time, a remarkable show of awareness among various Christian bodies of the great issues of human life that concern us all. However, the initiative here lies especially in Jewish circles, and why should those initiatives not lie there?

For example, if I were a Negro this morning, and not necessarily marching in Montgomery, but a professional Negro with a good position, who wanted to purchase a house in the suburbs of Chicago, I would not go to Deerfield--I would go to Glencoe because my chances of getting a hearing there would be much better. There is an open-occupancy ruling in Glencoe, something very markedly absent in Deerfield. Glencoe is predominantly Jewish; Deerfield, predominantly Christian. This, although an extreme example of the situation I am trying to alert you to, is the point at issue. The idea that we as Christians ought to be more tolerant because we have been told to love all men, even those who are unlovely and unlovable, seems patronizing. This is the first step, to be sure, and one that is not being taken in so many instances; but merely this and nothing more hardly does justice to the meaning and function of this faith in our common society.

I had a student last fall who came to us with a theological degree from another seminary. He entered a special seminar that I was giving on Ethics and the Old Testament, the biblical approach to society. As I was outlining some of the issues involved in relating biblical concepts and demands to present social issues, he remarked, "But the Jew is full of pride in this whole matter of society, nation, and culture." I asked him, "What do you mean?" He answered, "I have been trained in a dogmatic tradition which seems to deny the interpretation you are giving to the biblical answer to social problems." What he meant by this statement was

87

that for the Jew there remains this concern to build a Kingdom of God in history. What he intended was the same idea of what historical theology has meant by this distinction between Law and Gospel.

The Jew lives by Law to attain a social result. This fact, however, had not been emphasized in this student's training. He did not see religion as a social process. For the first time I began to see, from a ᵀewish point of view, that the matter of Law is not something that is merely a manifestation of ceremonial legalism. I maintain this point despite the fact that the legal dimension of Judaism has always been easily disposed of as an evil, especially in Protestantism. Rather, for the Jew, because of his eschatological outlook, Law is the way in which man performs the will of God. For Christians to talk about the hubris of the Jew is a very delicate business, if not an offense, for in the history of Jewish-Christian relations the shoe has often been on the other foot. Christianity has been far from clean of such ceremonial and ethical legalism.

I now would like to quote from a text, the likes of which can be found in many theological textbooks, at least in Protestant seminaries. This quotation comes from a book entitled « Old Testament Theology », Volume I, by Gerhard von Rad. Discussing Hebrew aesthetics, which he does in a magnificent fashion, von Rad makes a critical error in interpreting Judaism historically. He says: "Admittedly, as far as we can see, Israel lacked all critical reflection on the phenomenon of beauty--she persisted in standing right down to the last in sheer naive experience." (Italics mine.) Now what I am talking about here is not the "sheer naive experience" which was an undeniable ingredient of Israel's life--for this, in my judgment, is a credit to Israel's sense of the continuity between experience and thought. The break between reason and experience never really occurred for the Jews; their understanding of beauty never became the philosophical abstraction it did for the Greeks. The matter I am pressing here is that "she persisted in standing right down to the last." The "last" of which von Rad speaks was, of course, the birth and mission of Jesus. The "last" was the beginning of the Christian era. That was also the end of Judaism as a "living religion." Von Rad never thought about this matter when he wrote those words. He, like most Christians, felt that was the end: Judaism ended when Christianity began.

To those who are Catholic, I would suggest that you refer to the magnificent « Atlas of the Bible » by Professor Grollenberg. There, in the last sentence of the section on the Old Testament, you will find much the same attitude expressed in its own way.

Whether one uses the term "completed" or "last" or "fulfilled" or "ended," this, I submit, is the unexpressed assumption in Christian theological textbooks, literature, and educational materials in general: Christians <u>assume</u> that Judaism is superfluous as a living religion, and has been so for the last two thousand years.

TEN

Panel talk on curriculum: anti-Semitism and the early Church Fathers

William LeSaint, S.J.

Prefect of the Pontifical Faculty
St. Mary of the Lake Seminary, Mundelein, Illinois

I suppose that the first question a Patrologist has to ask himself, when he is dealing with the subject of anti-Semitism in a seminary classroom, is this: Were the Fathers of the Church anti-Semitic? I am afraid he will have to say that they were. I think that anti-Semitism is a part of the Christian tradition, and the Fathers were among the chief witnesses to tradition in the early centuries of the Church's history. I think, then, that we must acknowledge the existence of a definite anti-Semitism among the Fathers of the Church.

However, there are some distinctions which need to be made. First of all, there is a distinction between theological and social anti-Semitism, a distinction which has already been made in the conference by speakers who contrasted essential and practical anti-Semitism. Theological, or essential, anti-Semitism (Rabbi

Sandmel calls it axiomatic anti-Semitism) is found in all of the
Fathers of the Church. The early Christians said that Jesus of
Nazareth was the Messiah; this the Jews denied. Accordingly,
the Fathers of the Church thought of the Jews as essentially anti-
Christian, and of themselves not so much as anti-Semitic as anti-
anti-Christian.

Social anti-Semitism (nontheological or nonessential) is characterized by prejudice and persecution and ignorance and fear and
hatred and calumny and the teaching of contempt. Jules Isaac defines
it as "anti-Jewish prejudice; feelings of suspicion, contempt, hostility and hatred for Jews--both those who are merely of Jewish
parentage, and those who follow the Jewish religion."[1] We must
confess that this kind of anti-Semitism is also found in a number
of the Fathers of the Church; but again a distinction is necessary.
We find much more of this among the later Fathers than we do
among earlier writers. It is especially conspicuous during the
fourth century. John Chrysostom, of course, is notorious, and
one finds it difficult to repeat his vicious, slanderous remarks
about the Jews.[2] His language is inexcusable, and no effort should
be made to excuse it. His is not theological anti-Semitism, but
rather anti-Christian anti-Semitism. There is some controversy
as to the anti-Semitism of St. Augustine. At the Oxford Patristic
Conference, a year or so ago, one of the few occasions when the
atmosphere became somewhat charged was during a discussion
which took place after a paper on this subject.

During the earlier Patristic period, let us say during the second
century, there is evidence of anti-Semitism, but here a subdis-
tinction (if I may use scholastic terminology) needs to be made. At
Alexandria, and in schools influenced by Alexandria, we find considerable non-theological anti-Semitism. Origen, for example, in
the « Contra Celsum » shows a definite animus. It has often been
pointed out, however, that there was a tradition of vulgar, vicious
anti-Semitism at Alexandria for many years before the introduction
of Christianity there.

Elsewhere, during this period, we find a disposition to discuss
the theological issues without appealing to emotions or prejudice.
One of the earliest Christian treatises on this subject, written about
the middle of the second century, is Justin's « Dialogue with Trypho »
(probably the Rabbi Tarphon). In this discussion the adversaries
treat each other with great respect and courtesy. Justin speaks of
the salvation of both Jews and Christians, and he speaks of the
writings of the Old Testament with love and reverence. At one
point in the « Dialogue » the protagonists indicate a desire to

get off by themselves, away from the boisterous enthusiasm of their followers, so that they will be better able to talk over their differences quietly and objectively.[3] Justin is sometimes spoken of as an anti-Semitic writer. Essential anti-Semitism is there, but I cannot concur with the judgment that he is guilty of the kind of practical, social anti-Semitism which we now so much deplore.

The same is to be said of Tertullian's « Adversus Iudaeos »; and this is especially significant in an author of whom it is said that he always writes like an angry man. Tertullian insists that the only basic issue between Christians and Jews is this: Was Jesus the Messiah? He spends no time on name-calling, but is concerned almost exclusively with an examination of the Scripture texts which he considers relevant to the central point in dispute.

In conclusion, let me answer the two questions which have been put to me as a member of this panel. First: What is being done in the seminary Patrology course to help students clarify their thinking on the subject of anti-Semitism? I must confess that in the twenty-five years I have been teaching Patrology in a Roman Catholic seminary, the subject of anti-Semitism has rarely, if ever, come up. It is the feeling of our Patrologists that this topic is best left to the professors of Scripture and Moral Theology. This is the de facto situation. As to the second question--What can and should be done about anti-Semitism in the Patrology course?--it occurs to me that the best contribution which professors of Patristics can make is simply to tell their students what the Fathers of the Church actually had to say about the Jews. We must stress that nontheological anti-Semitism, as I have described it earlier, is evil and anti-Christian wherever it is found, whether in the writings of the Fathers or anywhere else. Essential, or axiomatic, anti-Semitism always has been and, in my view, always will be a part of the Christian tradition.

Before closing these brief remarks, there is one further point I have wanted to make during this panel discussion. The « Roman Martyrology », I believe, is still read in many Catholic seminaries. I am happy to say this practice is no longer followed at Mundelein. The « Martyrology » is an historically inaccurate compilation of the lives of the saints, and badly in need of revision. In some half-dozen places there are anti-Semitic passages of the most objectionable kind. It is to be hoped that in the revision of the « Martyrology » these passages will be deleted. Until they are deleted, authorities in Roman Catholic seminaries should certainly see to it that they are not read to the students in their institutions.

1 Jules Isaac, The Teaching of Contempt, p. 21.
2 See especially the eight Homilies against the Jews.
3 Justin, Dialogue with Trypho, ch. 9.

ELEVEN

Panel talk on curriculum:
anti-Semitism and Christian ethics

Richard A. McCormick, S.J.
Professor of Moral Theology
Bellarmine School of Theology, Loyola University

May I begin my statement concerning anti-Semitism and Christian ethics by pointing out to you that I speak as a moral and systematic theologian and that the views I express here today represent my thinking alone; I do not speak for all Catholic seminaries. What we should do in attempting to confront the problem of anti-Semitism in one seminary will perhaps become clearer as I attempt to describe what we are actually doing.

Let us turn to the first question: What are we actually doing in the seminary classroom regarding the subject of anti-Semitism? From the point of view of a systematic and moral theologian in the area of Christian ethics, we have restricted our efforts primarily to creating general attitudes and frames of mind. We meet the problem of anti-Semitism quite indirectly by creating certain nuances of value. By way of illustration of this approach to the problem, I might mention that the starting point of Catholic moral theology is the doctrine of baptism, our incorporation into the death and resurrection of Christ. This dedication to lead the Christ-life following the initiation of baptism may be expressed in the single term "charity." I do not mean by this that one models his life according to any Golden Rule or humanitarian principle. Rather, I intend it in a vigorous Pauline sense--an unfolding of the Christ-life in this world.

The remainder of moral theology is regarded as simply an explication, a concretization of this basic moral commitment to a life of charity, to love of God and love of neighbor for God's sake. For example, the concrete problems involving one's personal integrity, physical integrity, psychic integrity, in addition to problems of modern business, economics, surgery, etc.-- these are simply attempts to state clearly the minimal demands of love. Such a climate, where justice prevails over injustice, will hopefully establish a minimally acceptable climate for the Christian relationship between men. The situation which encourages and promotes justice for all persons serves, for our purposes, as an explication of the Christian principle of charity. This is the basic attitude we attempt to create among our students in the seminary; and we believe that it will inevitably touch the problem of anti-Semitism, though obliquely and indirectly.

More particularly, we would touch upon this problem in several areas of our moral treatises. First of all, when we discuss religious liberty as a corollary of the treatment of conscience, we meet obvious ramifications of the problem of anti-Semitism. Yet I am sure that in many cases the rather obvious applications of this teaching on religious liberty (and I intend this in the fullest sense of the term) are not made with respect to the problem of anti-Semitism. We do attempt, at any rate, to envision those applications of the principle of religious liberty as are basic to a healthy relationship between religious bodies of varying religious convictions.

Secondly, we would touch upon the problem of anti-Semitism when dealing with relationships between Catholics and non-Catholics insofar as these relationships involve us in communal worship. In Scholastic terms, this is the treatise on communicatio in sacris. We do have an ideal opportunity at this juncture to meet and effectively deal with the problem of interfaith relationships, and I think I can say honestly that we are availing ourselves of this opportunity, to some extent at any rate.

You may know that for many years there existed a rather apologetic, defensive attitude toward the matter of dialogue with other faiths. For many years we regarded this type of communication, above all else, as a danger to the security of the faith of the Catholic. Now, however, we seem to be approaching it (and rightly so) as much more a situation where each party involved in the conversation bears witness to his own faith. If I were to phrase this new attitude in a formula, I might say that we now view this type of association not so much as a contact with the faith of a person but, rather, with a person of another faith. This is unquestionably a basic and profound change in attitude among many Catholic churchmen, and it will affect in many ways the question of anti-Semitism.

Thirdly, the entire problem of prejudice, discrimination, and segregation is, of course, a matter which deserves, and indeed demands, a great deal more attention from moral theologians than it has received in the recent past. We have treated these problems in a most general way, and I am afraid that our application of the ethical principles of Christian theology has been limited to the area of the Negro problem, to the exclusion of other minority groups in America. To that extent, therefore, we have failed to apply our own principles in an area where they badly need application.

Another most encouraging change in our method of teaching moral theology is the introduction of the covenant structure of the moral life. This is a matter to which we should have been giving much attention; but moral theology, in the last couple of centuries, has not had a very happy career. The principle drawback which has affected moral theology has been the presence of a dominant casuistic element; we have experienced a kind of ethical unilaterialism. We are, however, returning increasingly to a biblical rootage in our moral teaching. This new movement among moral theologians cannot help but bring us more closely and explicitly into contact with the problem of anti-Semitism.

Now, what is to be done or what should we be doing in our seminaries in general and in my own field of moral theology to deal more adequately with the problem of anti-Semitism? We may approach the problem, I believe, from either one of two points of view. The first approach is what we might call "from then." I mean to suggest that we could approach the problem of anti-Semitism by utilizing a strictly theological, biblical approach, by showing the rootage of Christianity in Judaism, and by trying to establish the continuity of the Judeo-Christian tradition in the moral sphere. Do not misunderstand me. I refer here not to something unique to the past, but to an existing contemporary tradition involving real people. This is one approach that I am suggesting, from the inside out or from the "then, " so to speak.

The opposite tactic--which is now being applied in the matter of Negro and white relationships in this country but which, it seems to me, is equally applicable to any interracial or inter-faith problem--I would place under the title of "from now." According to this approach, we would deal with the problem in terms of the contemporary, cultural factors which underlie the total problem, rather than from a study of any biblical basis or any particular theology. In studying these contemporary prejudices and any other sociological factors relevant to the problem, we would ask the questions: What is the nature of the problem we now face? What are the facts before us? What are the sociological, psychological, cultural, and historical factors which constitute the present situation; how are they interrelated? With these questions as pivotal points, we would then use the concepts and methods of psychology, sociology, etc., to understand more intimately the situation as we confront it today.

Although I have given you only a simple picture of the options open to us in our seminaries, I feel that a forceful statement of the problem is of utmost importance. The reason for this is that we are dealing here with a problem of irrelevance. Anti-Semitic attitudes exist at the very core of Christianity. We recognize them, and yet, really, we do little or nothing to remedy these attitudes. We do not seem to confront these attitudes as pressing and relevant problems.

This lack of awareness and state of irrelevancy is what I sense to be my main difficulty in the seminary. Unfortunately, a mere exchange of professors in the fields of theology or biblical studies is not likely to remedy this situation. I fear, also, that my own interest, my own reading, and my own attempt to express convictions as a way to destroy whatever prejudice exists in my own heart will be such a small drop that I would be unable to dramatize the problem so as to make my students aware of the pressing needs of the situation.

I would suggest that what we need to solve this problem--and I confess that I do not know how to go about effecting this procedure-- is a vivid and unforgettable dramatization of the problem as it exists. The problem of discrimination, prejudice, and segregation against the American Negro--long a part of our American heritage-- was brought to national attention only by a courageous act of public dramatization. It is this kind of radical and unexpected breakthrough that we need to experience in connection with the problem of anti-Semitism. If we continue simply to make reflective statements, the problem will continue to be irrelevant and largely ignored by our students.

TWELVE

Panel talk on curriculum:
extension work in Israel

Richard N. Longenecker

Associate Professor of New Testament History and Theology
Trinity Evangelical Divinity School, Deerfield, Illinois

Our topic concerns what we are doing and what can be done in the seminaries regarding anti-Semitism. Distinctive to the school with which I am associated is a program founded in 1957 that I would like to mention, for it indicates our interest and reflects something of our reactions and efforts. This is the American Institute of Holy Land Studies (formerly called the Israel-American Institute), which is directed by Dr. G. Douglas Young, the former dean of our divinity school and presently professor of Old Testament. I wish that Dr. Young were here to speak of the program himself; but he is in Israel at the present time, and so I will speak for him.

The American Institute of Holy Land Studies is an attempt to carry on a graduate program on a year-round basis in Jerusalem in cooperation with the Hebrew University. Half of the course work is taken at the Institute in Jerusalem (while the student is learning modern Hebrew preparatory to entering classes at the Hebrew University), and half at the Hebrew University. The M.A. degree is awarded in cooperation with the Hebrew University.

During the first semester, professors from the Hebrew University teach a full schedule of courses at the Institute. In the past, Hebrew has been taught by Menahem Ragev, Aharon Rosen, and Chaim Schachter; comparative religions, by David Flusser, Chaim Wardi, and Raphael Werblowsky. Of interest in the latter area is the course on Christian Church history from the Jewish perspective, taught by Mr. Wardi, who is also counselor on Christian Affairs to the Ministry of Religious Affairs of the Government of Israel. Professor Werblowsky usually teaches two courses of special interest to our students: a course in Jewish thought from Ezra to the present, and a course in Biblical prophecy from the Jewish perspective. Geography is taught by Moshe Kochavi and Anson Rainey; archaeology, by Johanan Aharoni, Trude Dothan, and Yigael Yadin.

The Institute is registered with the Israeli Government through the Hebrew University, and its quarterly journal is edited by Mr. Wardi and published by the Government Printing Office.

While the Institute is not officially an extension of our seminary, its director comes from our ranks and some of our professors are on its board. We consider it our special interest, and our students are strongly urged to take advantage of the opportunities it affords.

The purpose of the American Institute of Holy Land Studies is, first of all, to function as a graduate school giving qualified American students opportunity to study in Israel under Israeli professors in the fields of Hebrew, archaeology, comparative religions, and Biblical studies--though, of course, to pursue their studies as Christians from within a Christian setting and environment. The Christian director of the Institute acts more as an overseas chaplain to the students than as professor.

Secondly, the Institute states frankly that it is interested in intercultural relations, with emphasis on the understanding of the Jew and appreciation of the nation Israel. I might add that Dr. Young, its director, is very definitely "philo-Semitic"; in fact, as his frequent public appearances with Mrs. Maier would indicate, I believe he would appreciate being called "Zionist."

Thirdly, the Institute's purpose is to promote dialogue, feeling that the Christian student has much to learn from the Jew (as Dr. Davies pointed out yesterday) and that, conversely, the Christian has something to say to the Jew--that there is a need for Jews to meet Christians who respect them for what they are and yet who recognize the distinctiveness of their own Christian faith.

Admittedly, there is a missionary thrust here. Such, it seems to me, is inevitable wherever men meet in dialogue holding differing views on matters of importance. Where there is conversation on significant issues, there is always the desire to convince--even, if I may use the word, to convert. Who of us is interested in dialogue on matters of ultimate concern that merely exchanges information?

However, this is not the sole reason for the Institute's existence--nor, I understand, even the primary one. To date, I've heard of no American students converting to Judaism, nor Jews (least of all Jewish professors) converting to Christianity. Yet the Institute is still judged by its board and its supporters to be a success, and this judgment is founded on the response of Christian students who have returned with a new appreciation of Judaism, of the Jew, of the nation Israel, and of their own Christian faith-- and a new dedication to Biblical studies. It is also judged a success on the basis of the experience of one of its students, Anson Rainey, who received such stimulation in the Institute that he continued his studies at the Hebrew University, received his doctorate at Brandeis University in the States, and is now a permanent resident in Israel teaching Semitic languages at the Tel Aviv branch of the Hebrew University.

The Institute also carries on activities of a cultural nature here at home, in the Evanston, Highland Park, and Deerfield areas. It sponsors cultural events that are presented and attended by both Christians and Jews. These have been frequently reported via local news media, and thus I won't report further here.

What then is being done in our seminary? Well, in addition to the usual courses in the seminary curriculum that bear on the history of Israel and the theology of Judaism, this program is in effect. Probably its greatest contribution to our seminary has to do with attitudes that are formed. As the Institute's director returns to teach in our school for one semester of each year, as professors have opportunity to come into contact with living Jews, and as students return to complete their education after a year in Israel, a climate of opinion is being formed within the seminary.

What can be done to form the minds of seminarians regarding Judaism and the Jew? I would assert that the major factor has to do with attitude.

We need to develop in our seminaries men who have depth of conviction (not just willing to find the happy medium, as it were), yet breadth of sympathy; men who have strong convictions (even convictions regarding legitimacy), yet who realize their own fallibility; men who recognize the centrality of Christ in the program of God, yet who also recognize that religious pluralism itself is under the Divine decree--and that includes the continued existence of Judaism as being by Divine directive.

Although I realize that it was not too well received, I must say that I appreciated the clarification of Professor Davies yesterday (which Father LeSaint likewise proposed this morning) with regard to the distinction between anti-Semitism and anti-Judaism. It is possible to be anti-Judaic, and yet, realizing our own fallibility, recognizing the fact of religious pluralism, and respecting the freedom of the conscience, not be anti-Semitic. I would propose that Christianity is inherently anti-Judaic, but I would likewise strenuously insist that that does not make it anti-Semitic per se.

Particularism has been soundly thrashed in the sessions of yesterday. Personally, I am not at all sure that it can be identified as a primary factor in the rise of anti-Semitism; though, when combined with other factors, it can be disastrous. The factors involved in ethnocentricism need to be more carefully spelled out; and these are seldom primarily religious in nature.

Trinity Evangelical Divinity School, the institution I represent, has a high degree of particularism in its theology--but not, I trust, exclusivism. We are not ready to box in the sovereign God to our understanding of what we believe to be His normative order. We believe we have some appreciation of the Divine will, but we are not ready to turn this into some new gnostic system or to begin playing God in judgment of others. As the name of our sponsoring denomination would suggest (Evangelical Free Church of America), we lay great emphasis on the concepts of religious liberty, the legitimacy of religious pluralism, the freedom of conscience, and the fallibility of all men (though we, like others, do not always act as if we believe such); and we have no expressed negative attitudes toward the Jew as a Christ-killer (who of us would not and has not done the same?).

This may sound to some to be paradoxical, antithetical, and even anachronistic. Yet we believe that we can demonstrate the possibility of combining depth of conviction and breadth of appreciation. We are not ready to talk about relativity of truth, but we are certainly prepared to recognize relativity of understanding because of human fallibility--on the part both of ourselves and of others.

In this matter of anti-Semitism, the student learns more from attitudes than from proscribed course content. And attitudes in the areas of racial and social concern cannot be traced back to the issues of religious particularism or universalism. That is too simple! These may be factors, and they may be used in explanation of prejudices formed on other bases; but often they have very little direct influence. Attitudes of a proper sort must be exemplified in our seminaries if we are to turn out truly educated men. And that is our task as teachers.

THIRTEEN

Judeo-Christian themes: conflicts and complements

Joseph Sittler
Professor of Theology
The Divinity School, University of Chicago

During the long course of preparation for this Conference I asserted that we should most rightly honor the gravity of the issues
that bring us together by a preliminary effort, following the more
reportorial statements and discussions, to specify the great themes
that lie at the center of the deepest difference between Israel and
the Church. I did not suppose then, and do not now, that we should
have the time nor I the competence to undertake a very full explication of this difference. But I am convinced that the effort must
begin, not only by a continuation of the steady body of literature that
deals with this difference in scholarly books and monographs, but
by face-to-face dialogue.

As so often happens in such Committees, the voice that articulates
a point is saddled with the responsibility to undertake the task. And
the first point I must make is that the issue is not rightly approached

if we ask that themes in Christian theology are generative of anti-Semitic attitudes. Such an approach, while able, to be sure, to designate some of these, could do little more. Such an approach would assume that we intimately know one another, have interior and accurate knowledge of the structural context in which certain affirmations are made, are completely clear about the intended substance of these--and have only to resolve to modify the vigor of their pronouncement or stifle our mutual sense of their centrality.

That entire assumption is totally false. Our problem is a defect in knowledge, an inadequate religious apprehension of the confessional intentions of our several teachings, and a mutual inability or refusal to peer into and honor the organic integrity and multifaceted interior relationship that constitute what might be called a teaching and confessing system.

Having put the problem that way, I am certain of two things: that it is rightly put, and that I can go only a modest distance toward the exposure of what I have formally put.

But a beginning must be made--and for purposes of what I hope will be a long and clarifying discussion following upon this brief paper, I submit the following propositions.

(1) The knowledge of God is differently understood in Israel and in the Church.

The God of Israel became known to her in historical care for her--and that conviction of care is the root of Israel's self-understanding as the elect of God. The deliverance from Egypt is in Israel's tradition a primal and vast paradigm of an acting God who in mercy, power, and judgment liberated a people forward to his purpose. This paradigmatic deliverance resonates through Israel's history in recollecting and celebrating life as the inner meaning and force whereby she is a people of God that shall not die--for God has acted, given his covenant, and in the Law made known his way.

Israel's knowledge of God is relentlessly "factic," nonmetaphysical, bound to the revelation of God in history. This center and source and continuing activity of the revealing God is what lies back of and under Israel's insistence upon the oneness of God. The term is not to be understood fundamentally as a mathematical insistence; that is presupposed. The term points rather to the unmodifiable singularity of that Creator who is the awful ground and power and governor of all that is. An understanding of the working of the Glory is essential to a comprehension of Israel's intention in her praise of the one God; and the mind, even the religious mind, that does not start there in its effort to listen to Israel is stopped at all imaginable other starting places.

The knowledge of God in the Christian Community has classically affirmed the same center. But in the development of Christian theology an epistemological symbiosis has so complicated this affirmed center that our present speech to one another about the knowledge of God has got to make its way among accumulated difficulties of enormous size and number. When, for instance, Père Danielou writes a little book, « The Ways of Knowing », he discloses that in the intellectual tradition of the Church an incessant and dismayingly sophisticated counterpoint with the philosophers of the various cultures within which the Church has lived her life was manifested in her earliest reflections about herself, her Lord, and about God, and has never ceased. A single illustration. When Professor Paul Tillich speaks of Philosophy of Religion he chooses, works out, and draws conclusions from an alliance with a venerable ontological position; and when Abraham Heschel writes a « Philosophy of Judaism » he does no such thing! He uses the term "philosophy" to designate and mark out the basic spheres of human concern, the enduring issues of life, and in an orderly and sequential way he addresses these out of the Godly, historically learned and transmitted vitalities of Israel's faith. The philosophies are known but not utilized; for no philosophy can, except negatively, celebrate the Glory.

(2) The relation of God to history is differently understood in Israel and in the Church.

For Israel the reality, presence, power, mercy, judgment of God, is identical with the place of his revelation--in time and space. Just as God is one, so he is relentlessly historical. Israel's "world" is monodimensional--for God is the Creator. Just as history is the theater of his revelation, so history alone is the theater of his "being" his consummating purpose, the place of his intention-realized. Israel has an "eschatology" to be sure; but in order to specify its particularity the word would be spelled with a lower case e! For Israel's hope, her sense of boundary, her sense of the sphere of God's power, mercy, fulfillment, is radically historical.

Israel's faith does not have its genesis in history, but it has there its reality and its hope. God alone is the source of faith; history alone is the realm of faith. It is thus clear why Israel is the people of hope, a people that waits in history for the ultimate working out of God's purpose, the establishment of his kingdom, the vindication of his Glory.

How this radicality of the absolute relation of God and history forms organically the praise, and hope, and faith-dimensions of the two communities is dramatically set forth in the rite that marks the reception of a new child into the tradition of each. Both circumcision and baptism acknowledge the priority of God and the genesis of all gifts in him. Neither the child of Israel nor the child of the Church is, in his own knowledge or will, the interpretive center of the rite. In both cases God's gratia preveniens is acknowledged and celebrated with joy. But Israel's child at his beginning, as at his ending, is placed within the people of God's care and promise, and has there, in history and in history's continuity of the people that cannot die, his blessedness. In this act time is not fractured; "dispensations" of God's presence are not multiplied; earth and heaven, time and eternity, are not set over against each other.

In a Christian baptism, however, for all that is one with Israel, another dimension of fulfillment is assumed; "a dying and a rising" with God's servant, the Church's Lord, is declared. The prefatory prayer in the Book of Common Prayer has the phrase "that this child may enjoy the everlasting benediction of the heavenly washing, and may come to the eternal kingdom which thou hast promised by Christ our Lord."

(3) The intention of the doctrine of the Holy Trinity must be broken loose from its imprisonment in forms of its explication in the Church's history and reformulated in such ways as to protect its intention against the denials, repudiations, and reductions which it can be understood, by Israel's faith, to have effected. There are some forms of trinitarian doctrine which are as bewildering to contemporary Christians as they are repellant to Israel.

By the doctrine of the Holy Trinity, Christians centrally mean to affirm the holiness, mercy, revelation, presence, of the one God of Abraham, Isaac, and Jacob. But they have encountered in an historical event, so they confess, the concreted presence and salvatory reality of this one God, a presence who was himself of "the root of Jesse." This present and effective and historical one understood himself absolutely the servant, the effective presence of the power, of the one God--the Father. He presented himself as an historical transparency to Israel's God--and violently repudiated any estimation of himself that in any sense compromised the oneness of God.

Trinitarian doctrine is an effort to do justice to the one God; and when it speaks of the "modes of his presence" or of Christ as "being of one substance with the Father," the intention is to praise

107

the mercy and the merciful ingenuity of the one God who would be and became God-for-us as Father, as historical embodiment as Son, and as abiding, fructifying Spirit. The intention of the doctrine is to enrich the doctrine and celebrate the power of God--not to split, or nullify, or modify the God of Israel's adoration.

A pressing necessity is not that this doctrine should be so fashioned as to be calculatedly acceptable to Israel. The proper business of the Church, and of all her teaching institutions, is so to speak of trinitarian-intention as to put the issue aright. Idolatry is as blasphemous for Church as for Israel; but all trinitarian doctrinal explication does not clearly enough say what it means as to avoid the charge.

FOURTEEN

Jewish-Christian relations
and the seminary: comments

John J. Egan

Director, Office of Urban Affairs
Catholic Archdiocese of Chicago

I am honored that I have been invited here to speak to you, and the only justification I can personally have for speaking to you tonight is that I firmly believe what the Bishops in Rome decreed last year when they said: "Because the human race today is growing more and more into a civic, economic and social unity, it is so much the more necessary that the clergy, by combined effort and aid, wipe out every kind of separateness so that the whole human race may be brought into the unity of the family of God."

A small, objectively unimportant incident occurred in my life a week ago Sunday night which epitomizes for me the new and closer relationships which must exist between the various faiths in our society today. The Reverend Edward Reddick (a Presbyterian minister), Rabbi Robert Marx, and I met in a radio control room where we were to make a broadcast together. The three of us had just returned separately from the unique and vivid experience of participating in a very small way with the people of Selma, Alabama, in their quest for freedom. No words were spoken, but in the clumsy way men do, we warmly embraced one another out of mutual love, respect, and concern.

I have been asked to speak tonight about a few points relative to the new forms of relationships which must occur between members of the differing faiths and how they relate to the seminary. I would humbly ask the men who are here from Mundelein Seminary, if they are perplexed by some of the things I say tonight, that, out of charity and not out of equity, they would not confer with me or that they do not look up my seminary record.

It would seem to me that all young men emerging from their training in seminary life today must have amongst so many other things a knowledge of the current trends in Protestantism, Judaism, and Catholicism, as well as an understanding of the best that each religious tradition and current scholarship has to offer. What I mean here is that the Roman Catholic and Protestant seminarian must not only know the Old Testament and Jewish history, insofar as this is possible in a crowded curriculum, but that he should also have some acquaintance with the Jewish theological mind of today in its several developments. Allow me to be more specific.

(1) We should admit that up to now we have done practically nothing academically with respect to the problem of Jewish-Christian relationships. We should admit this frankly. Most of us, even those who have some scholastic pretensions, do not even know what has been written on the question. We know nothing of the history of the question. If we were to investigate, we would find that although much has been written, there is still much to be written. Some of this writing could be cooperative--as a Christian-Jewish dialogue.

(2) There should be a clear definition of the problem or problems of Jewish-Christian relations. Perhaps an academic committee composed of rabbis, priests, university men of both faiths, etc., could be established to define these problems.

(3) Another important area of investigation would be the determination of the differences of various Christian groups in their relationships to Judaism. How do the individual Christian sects differ in their relationships to Judaism, and in what way is that relationship affected by their relationships with one another?

(4) Eventually there might be a professor of Jewish studies in Christian seminaries, or such departments might well be set up. Even now there are professors of Protestant theology and chairs

of Roman Catholic studies in Catholic and Protestant universities respectively.

(5) Interseminary contact should not take place just between Christians, but also between all Christian sects and Jewish theological schools. These discussions should be open-ended, at least in the beginning, that is, they should aim at mutual understanding and mutual cooperation in various community projects both academic and social.

(6) It must be emphasized that interfaith lines of communication will not open up unless there first is freedom of communication in the particular seminary wanting to make contact with another sect or religion.

(7) Christian-Jewish dialogue obviously presents a greater challenge than intra-Christian dialogue. Let us admit this frankly and move from there.

(8) Let us stress our points of agreement. We have a common theological heritage. There is a great deal of agreement in the area of mores and social action. There are obvious beginnings for both academic and social cooperation.

It should be hoped that the intrafaith study and action program suggested above will help open lines of communication with and within particular Christian sects. My experience tells me that the most obvious thing the seminary must do is to drive deep down into the mind and person of the young man preparing for the ministry the willingness and the openness to accept, to love, and to respect all persons of other faiths--particularly when they share the same personal life commitment for the redemption of the people of God.

This may sound to the scholars who are assembled here and to leaders in seminary training as rather trite and all too obvious. I would only respond that the neglect of this attitude and response is today all too obvious and all too tragic in its extension among the clergy of all faiths in our metropolitan areas. We have not yet succeeded in teaching our seminarians the meaning of the human encounter. We have preached and practiced a disincarnate love which I find, in our neighborhoods in Chicago, often refuses or does not condescend to accept a clergyman of another faith as a person who shares the same travail and concern over the spiritual, social, and cultural misery in which many of our people find themselves today.

May I be so bold as to submit to you from my experience that while the work which you have begun and will continue on the highest level of academic scholarship is crucial to our under-ing of our past and also of our present position, until the clergy in our neighborhoods learn to speak and act with each other as human beings mutually concerned with the welfare of the people of God, your work, in spite of its academic value, will not find roots in the churches and synagogues of the United States.

What I am pleading for here is that our seminaries do everything possible to teach love and respect for others to the young men being trained today. And I submit that seminary students will not learn this unless they learn to know and communicate with other people and, particularly, other seminarians of different faiths. In view of the winds of ecumenical change which are blowing across the world today, if our seminarians do not learn to speak to one another while in the seminary, if they continue to live in isolation and meet one another only through the objections and the syllogisms and the theses of their classrooms, in short, if they grow up as strangers to one another, they will continue as strangers to their conferees in the ministry in the midst of their people.

Finally, I would like to tell you tonight that, from our experience in Chicago, the close relationships of so many members of our differing faiths have only been forged by the mutual suffering, involvement, participation, and work which has resulted from our struggles to solve some of the social and human problems which face our community and our people. I claim, therefore, and it is my experience, that although discussions on theology and tradition are obviously useful and needed in themselves, this is not the place to start in our neighborhoods. It is when they are involved in fighting and struggling for the needs of their people, be they in housing, employment, race, youth, urban renewal, etc., that clergymen grow closer together.

We have no new form here in Chicago. What we do have is the extension of that which has occupied your attention for the last two days. Theological discussions in our neighborhoods among the several faiths have not as yet blossomed in depth, variety, or number. However, clergy of all faiths in many of the neighborhoods of Chicago know one another as brothers and share with one another their deepest aspirations, hopes, and difficulties. We have tried to assist one another and have grown to know and love each other in the breaking of the chains which prevent so many of the people in our inner city from living a full human life.

Out of community organization work and the unraveling of neighborhood problems has come in Chicago a brotherhood among the clergy which I believe is indispensable and the forerunner of creative theological discussion. We have a long way to go, but the embrace between the brilliant young rabbi, the zealous Negro Protestant minister, and myself in that radio control room last week convinced me that the path is easier than any of us sus-pected a few years ago.

FIFTEEN

Jewish-Christian relations and the seminary: comments

E. Spencer Parsons
Dean Elect
Rockefeller Memorial Chapel, University of Chicago

The first thought that comes to my mind with respect to Judaism and the Christian seminary is that I would be dishonest if I did not confess that twenty years ago when I was in the seminary, the religious life of Jews was not taken with any great degree of serious-ness. To the extent that we studied Judaism at all, it was largely in the context of sociology, history and archaeology. The stereo-type of the Jewish religion came to us, as seminarians, largely through eyes dimmed by the controversies of the first century of the Christian era.

I think I would want to say frankly that those of us who have been educated in Christian seminaries, as already alluded to by Monsignor Egan, have been unaware of the thought of Jewish theologians from biblical days to the present. Jewish theologians are largely unknown to Protestant scholars. To be sure, there are names like Abraham Heschel and Martin Buber which are familiar to Christian scholars. But other than these, the degree to which Protestant students in seminaries are really acquainted with their life and thought is tragically minimal.

As a Protestant minister, I think I would have to confess, in the context of the discussion here and with particular reference to Mr. Rosen's paper, that it is true that only occasionally have we Christians in America been truly sensitive to the persistence of anti-Semitism. Of course, we have been aware of it in the moments when it has expressed itself in gross injustice. However, I would suspect it is true that the seminary curriculum and maybe seminary life have been largely unaware of the subtleties of anti-Semitism and not sufficiently cognizant of the strange interrelationships between certain religious convictions and antisocial behavior.

Indeed, as a Christian, I think I want to explore further what it means when men and women say "no" to the acceptance of the Christian gospel, particularly with regard to its evangelical nature. I suspect that what begins to take place when one man says "no" to what another most deeply believes is an incipient--and, finally, a guarded but explicit--expression of hostility. In this regard, it would seem fair to say that Jews, for many Christians, are still a problem, even in the dialogic atmosphere in which they are presently involved. The fundamental problem is that we find it difficult to see Jews as persons when they stand in some sense, though delicately and graciously, in the position of "no" to the central affirmations of the Christian faith. This constitutes a part of the real situation in which we find ourselves. How to respect a "no" from any person takes a good deal of sophistication and understanding.

In recent years, certainly, the relationship between Christians and Jews has moved from one of aloofness and/or overt hostility to one in which there is serious conversation between us. I think it would not be unfair to characterize the many interfaith conversations that took place in my early days as a university pastor in Cambridge, Massachusetts, as primarily sociological, anthropological and cultural in nature. Only in recent years, and actually in very recent years, have such conversations been rooted fundamentally in the biblical tradition and in terms of the logical structures of the various religious traditions.

Amos Wilder, in his paper which was read and submitted to this conference, wrote that the "primary interest will be in an encounter between Jews and Christians deeply committed to their respective revelations, covenants and ethical obligations."

The new fact of the ecumenical conversations that are taking place in our time is a new respect for particularity, and this is essential to real interpersonal relationships. Truth is not meaningful when all of its historic, concrete, and even peculiar characteristics, are vaporized into a mist of generalities. A Jew is no man in general, but a particular human being. For those of us rooted in an understanding of God which is radically conditioned by historical events, we must take each other in all of his particularities, accepting each other in his concreteness, even as we believe God has accepted us as we are.

In ≪ The Meaning of Revelation ≫, by H. Richard Niebuhr, a book which has been a pivotal point for my understanding of the nature of truth, I believe we find the clue. I have reference to that understanding of our own selves, either as Christian or Jew, as a vision which comes in large measure by virtue of what somebody else--standing in a different perspective--sees and understands when he confronts us and when we enter together into dialogue and encounter. We are as Christians not only what Christians say we are, but also what others who are not Christians say we are. Therefore, Jews are not simply what they are by virtue of their own internal confession, but they are also what they are by virtue of what others understand them to be.

Coming from New England, I have treasured with particular affection a sermon preached by Dr. Edwin Dahlberg, former President of the National Council of Churches, entitled "From the Other Side of Concord Bridge." The very title of this sermon establishes certain guidelines for dialogue. We must take seriously not only what God is always doing everywhere and at all times, but also what God has done in each of us in each of our experiences. The reality of God which is being disclosed to both of us in the dialogue is a reality which neither one of us could have comprehended alone. We must dare to believe that he who is the Father of us both has revealed something of himself and of his constant purpose in the mighty acts that he has wrought among his people. Therefore, I would hope that we shall at least be able to say as Christians, "Thank God for the disclosure of God in the history and in the life of the Jewish people, by which they come to know something of the same reality and life that we have known." And I would hope that Jews will soon be able to say with a fresh honesty, "Thank God for the disclosure of himself and his will and way in Jesus of Nazareth, whom the Christians name as their Lord, for he has disclosed to them something of the reality of the Father whom we also know."

I would hope further, in the spirit of this conference and particularly of the statements made this afternoon, that each of us could be a corrective to the other; that the Jew could be a corrective to a certain kind of specious Christology; that my Jewish friends could be a reminder to me that I must never become too fascinated with speculations about the otherworldly dimensions of human existence.

I would like to believe, in the providence of God, that I, as a Christian, am a reminder to my Jewish brethren that there are disclosures of reality outside the Law--disclosures which are deeply embedded not in logic, nor in systems of thought, nor in the generalities of experience, but even in the mystery of a single human individual. I would hope, as a Christian, that I might be a reminder to my Jewish friends that there are personal realities, in addition to corporate realities, that constitute a part of our religious life. I would hope that, by being a Christian, I might remind my Jewish friends that there are substantial realities which are unseen and eternal, which bring judgment to bear upon a too-great preoccupation with the structures and the spaces and the places of this world.

Finally, I would hope that the verbal categories of our traditions could be constantly recast, though remaining faithful to their fundamental meanings and to the realities to which they point. I believe that insofar as each of us continues to speak in our own traditional biblical language, Jews and Christians together must be deeply mindful that we are both in danger of mouthing some terribly irrelevant words.

SIXTEEN

Judaism and the
Christian seminary curriculum

Robert Gordis
Seminary Professor of Bible
Jewish Theological Seminary

The Conference which has brought us together is one of the most welcome signs of our times. It testifies eloquently to the desire to establish among the various branches of Western religion, not merely communication, but a community of true understanding and a mutual enrichment of the spirit.

This deep yearning for brotherhood found dramatic expression in the brief but blessed pontificate of John XXIII and in the living waters his activity has unfrozen. It is reflected in the history of the ecumenical movement in world Protestantism, which is so well illumined in the thoughtful and fair-minded paper of Professor Amos N. Wilder. It has another source in the deep concern for intergroup understanding as basic to the stability of the free society, now being challenged by redoubtable foes. This aspiration has led to the creation and maintenance of such interdenominational agencies as the National Conference of Christians and Jews and such Jewish agencies as the Anti-Defamation League of B'nai B'rith, the sponsor of this Conference.

I shall not attempt to summarize and evaluate the papers presented at this Conference. The richness of insight, the depth of learning, and above all, the wholehearted sincerity in the quest for truth which informs tham all, make them an invaluable re-source for developing a mature understanding of the relationship, both actual and ideal, between the two components of the Judeo-Christian tradition. How much my own presentation owes to these scholars and thinkers will become abundantly clear.

It is a self-evident truth that the philosophy of education cher-ished by any society represents its conception of the ideal future. For what the school seeks to realize is its vision of tomorrow, sufficiently close to the present to be capable of fulfillment, yet sufficiently better than the present to fire the hearts and minds of men. In asking what role Judaism should occupy in the Chris-tian seminary curriculum, we are in effect asking what attitude shall the mid-twentieth-century Western world adopt toward the Jewish heritage and its living exemplars. The parallel question as to what role a knowledge of Christianity should play in the training of rabbis would be entirely justified and is worthy of discussion on another occasion. As for the subject before us, it seems to me that the answer may be subsumed under four related yet distinct headings.

(1) Since full understanding of the Old
Testament is basic to a vital Christianity,
a knowledge of the three-thousand-year-old
tradition of biblical interpretation in Judaism
is an essential element.

Today it is clear to all true Christians that Marcionism in any of its forms is a fatal distortion of the Christian message and that Christianity cut loose from its roots in the Hebrew Scriptures would forfeit much of its truth and staying power. When the early Church rejected Marcionism as a heresy in the second century, it revealed its essential healthy-mindedness. In our day the bloody neo-Marcionism of Aryan Christianity in Nazi Germany has dem-onstrated that the attempt to divorce the Christian world-view from the Hebrew Scriptures is a heresy that is finally expiated in blood.

Moreover, what is needed is the full Old Testament, not an expurgated or abridged selection. In his learned paper, Professor William D. Davies has pointed out that modern scholarship under-

stands that the biblical heritage of Christianity is not restricted
to the prophets of Israel. In his words, "a deeper Jewish and
Christian understanding of the first century, often informed by
the agony of our time, has made it easier for us to do justice to
the legal tradition in Judaism." Now the Hebrew canon recognizes
a third section in the Hebrew Scriptures, by the side of the Torah
and the Prophets, the Hagiographa, which enshrines the products
of biblical wisdom. How much religious depth Christianity would
lose without the Psalms and how much narrower its intellectual
horizons would be without the books of Proverbs, Job, and Eccle-
siastes. It is the totality of the Hebrew Scriptures which calls
for understanding by the teachers and expounders of Christianity.

Now the Bible arose within the Jewish people, who have continued to study the Scriptures and to cultivate the Hebrew language in an unbroken tradition for three millennia. The fruits of
this far-flung activity are particularly important today, when a
greater degree of respect for the authenticity of the Masoretic
text has come into being among modern scholars. This attitude
is in part a natural reaction against the extreme vagaries of
nineteenth- and early-twentieth-century critical scholarship.
Until very recently it was customary to emend the Hebrew text
with great abandon and little humility and, I may add, with
little concern for the canons of sound scientific method, producing
a language best described as "German theological Hebrew,"
something strange and fearsome to behold. Today deeper re-
searches by contemporary biblical scholars, Catholic, Protestant,
and Jewish, a growing familiarity with ancient Oriental literature,
the discovery of the Dead Sea Scrolls with their far-reaching
implications for biblical studies--all these factors have given us
a higher appreciation of the essential validity of the transmitted
text.

Since this is so, the living tradition of biblical interpretation
in Judaism, which is to be found in rabbinic literature, in the
vast expanses of the Talmud and the Midrash, as well as among
medieval commentators and philologists, is no longer an out-
worn curiosity of the past. The insights arrived at by Jewish
biblical exegesis through the ages need to be rediscovered by
modern Christian scholars, who will be reviving an honorable
Christian tradition. They will be following in the footsteps of such
great predecessors as Origen, who in his stupendous Hexapla
collated all the extant Greek versions of the Hebrew Bible with
the Hebrew text and consulted Jewish scholars in Caeserea in his
vast work, and Saint Jerome, whose Vulgate was a massive ef-

fort to discover Hebraica veritas for the good of the Church and who frequently cited his Jewish teachers and rabbinic exegesis.

This tradition of scholarly collaboration continued, though with interruptions, through the Middle Ages in the great biblical and rabbinic scholars both in Protestantism and Catholicism: Egidio, Reuchlin, Munster, the Buxtorfs, and many more. Luther leaned so heavily upon the Latin commentaries of Nicholas de Lyra that the couplet circulated, "Si Lyra non lyrasset,/Luther non saltasset." But De Lyra's work was largely an epitome of the medieval Jewish commentator, Rashi. As a result, Luther's classic translation of the Bible into German has been described, with some exaggeration, as a German version of Rashi. The translators of the Authorized Version of 1611 leaned primarily upon the commentaries of another Jewish scholar, Rabbi David Kimhi. The works of these and other great medieval Jewish scholars, such as Abraham ibn Ezra and Abulwalid ibn Ganah, still possess rich treasures that are often overlooked. The great biblical commentaries of Franz Delitzsch owe not a little of their enduring value to his familiarity with medieval Jewish exegesis--a familiarity all but nonexistent in our age. Even today, when we are the beneficiaries of a growing knowledge of com-parative Semitic languages and of related disciplines, I believe it true to say that perhaps a large proportion of our best exegesis is embedded in the great medieval Jewish commentators and grammarians.

Moreover, Jewish biblical interpretation has continued unin-terruptedly to the present day. When this rich quarry is ignored, as Catholic exegesis was wont to be ignored in Protestant circles in the past and as American scholarship still tends to be overlooked overseas, the level of our common understanding of Holy Writ is gravely impoverished.

(2) Judaism has a second significant role to
play in the seminary curriculum in providing an
understanding of the background of Jesus, the
Apostles, Paul and the early Church.

There should be no need to labor the point that it was not biblical religion which nurtured the human career of Jesus, but rabbinical Judaism. We may pinpoint it further as being basically Pharisaic Judaism, the fundamental insights of which were accepted among virtually all Jews, with the exception of the Sadducees.

All the other sects in Second Temple Palestine carried one or another Pharisaic doctrine to extremes--or to its logical conclusion.

The Zealots, who with limited physical means fought against the Romans, were basically impatient Pharisees, unable to wait for God's own time to see the overthrow of Roman tyranny. The Essenes, who after nearly two thousand years of silence have begun to speak to us in their own words through the Dead Sea Scrolls and to whose circle John the Baptist probably belonged, emphasized the ideal of purity in its most radical form, a doctrine fundamental to the Pharisees, as their name "Separatists" indicates. The various Apocalyptic sects all stressed the Messianic faith which the Pharisees had enunciated. In their way of life, virtually all Jews followed the basic pattern laid down by the rabbinic sages.

This was true of the followers of Jesus as well, as the New Testament makes abundantly clear. Such basic elements of faith as the resurrection of the dead, the Messiah and the Kingdom of God, the primacy of the two commandments to love God and one's neighbor, without which Christianity is inconceivable, were all Pharisaic doctrines. The massive commentary on the New Testaof Strack-Billerbeck, as well as the writings of Abrahams, Schechter, Montefiore, Herford, and countless other scholars, has indicated the hundreds of points of contact between the earliest Christian circles of Jesus, of his disciples and followers, with Rabbinic Judaism. When Paul, whose background was radically different from that of Jesus, described himself as "a Pharisee son of a Pharisee" (Acts 23:6), he was underscoring the truth that it was a Rabbinic Judaism--modified, to be sure, in different circles and varying countries--which was the universal spiritual climate of world Jewry and the soil from which Christianity sprang.

Here the discovery of the Dead Sea Scrolls and the elucidation of their contents has wrought a veritable revolution in our understanding of the sources of Christianity.[1] Dismissing the extreme vagaries to which some scholars have fallen prey, we find a striking and totally unexpected implication emerging from these documents: Much of the content of early Christian thought and practice, previously thought to have its source in extra-Jewish circles, whether in Hellenistic thought or in the mystery religions, is now seen to emanate from the life and outlook of the Dead Sea Sectarians.

In the past it was generally believed that the faith and ethical teaching of Christianity were by and large Jewish in origin, while the theology and ritual of the Church represented the influence of Hellenistic religion and philosophy and Oriental mystery cults. This attitude was supported by the fact that parallels between

Jewish rabbinic sources and the New Testament were most plentiful for the Synoptic Gospels and much rarer for the Gospel of John and the Pauline Epistles. Now the Dead Sea Scrolls show most of their striking affinities of expression with the Fourth Gospel and the Epistles. Such elements as the boundless faith in the Righteous Teacher, the ideals of celibacy and of property held in common, the emphasis upon purity, the conflict between "the children of light" and "the children of darkness," the Messianic interpretation of scriptural passages, the communion meal of the faithful, which is a prototype of the Messianic banquet at "the end of days"--all these features of the early Christian Church are represented in our documents.

Thus much of the Gentile influence in Christianity is now seen not to be Gentile at all. In sum, the Christian debt to Judaism be-comes immeasurably enlarged, for it now includes both the main-stream of Normative Judaism and the lesser currents of Jewish sectarianism. The evidence for this relationship is so extensive that Dupont-Sommer has observed that it is a delicate question "to determine wherein and to what degree Christianity represents an original manifestation of the human spirit, a task to which theologians will feel impelled to address themselves."

It should be clear that when we describe Christianity as the offspring of Judaism, we are not denying or minimizing its own individuality. But to explore the nature of this relationship to Judaism and reveal the unique character of the Christian vision, a knowledge of Judaism from within, as well as of Christian life and thought, is required. Here the New Testament cannot serve as an all-sufficient source. The Gospels and the Epistles are the expression of an embattled Church fighting for its life, with all the passions, blind spots, and exaggerations that are the inevitable concomitants of conflict. The student and teacher of Christianity requires some first-hand knowledge of the great literary documents of Normative Judaism: the Mishnah, the Talmud, the Midrash. These are indispensable for a full understanding of the origins and development of Christianity.

The two aspects of Judaism that we have thus far discussed are essentially concerned with the past, though their implications for the present are far-reaching. The other aspects that are relevant to the Christian seminary curriculum are basically contemporary, though rooted in the past.

(3) The teacher and exponent of Christianity in
the modern world must, of necessity, possess
an understanding of Jews and Judaism as living
elements of the modern world and not as a
"fossilized relic of Syriac society," to cite
Toynbee's famous and unfortunate phrase.

Now Toynbee's utterance was a secularized version of a widespread religious theory. According to this view, Jews are
members of a petrified community which for two thousand years,
since the advent of Christianity, has shriveled up and lost all its
positive attributes except that of being a stiff-necked people.

In spite of the hoary antiquity of this doctrine, born of religious controversy centuries ago, I hope I shall be forgiven if I
suggest that its retention is not essential to Christian loyalty
and vitality. There is sufficient creative capacity within
Christian theology to evolve a conception of the role of the Jewish
people in the Christian world that will be more just and more kind.
This revision of outlook will be easier to achieve if the scholars
and teachers of Christianity achieve a perception of the true nature
of modern Judaism. For modern Judaism is not the vestigial remains
of Old Testament religion, though obviously rooted in it. To describe
Judaism within the framework of the Old Testament is as misleading
as a picture of contemporary American life in terms of the Constitution, which is, to be sure, the basic law of the land but far from
coextensive with our present legal and social system.

Modern Judaism is the product of a long and rich development
of biblical thought. It possesses a normative tradition embodied
in the Mishnah and the Talmud, as well as in the Responsa and the
Codes of the post-talmudic period. Nor is this all. By the side of
this dominant strand are the aberrant tendencies, sectarian and
heretical, that were never without influence and cannot be ignored.
These include the apocryphal and pseudepigraphal literature,
recently enriched--and complicated--by the sensational discovery
of the Dead Sea Scrolls. The Middle Ages, building upon their
biblical and talmudic antecedents, created the strands of philosophy,
mysticism, legalism, and Messianism, all of which contributed to
the character of modern Judaism. In the modern era, as every informed observer knows, the various schools--conventionally subsumed under the headings of Orthodoxy, Conservatism, and Reform-
do not begin to exhaust the variety of religious experience and at-
tidues to be found in the Jewish community.

In brief, modern Judaism in all its forms is not Biblical Judaism,
not even Talmudic Judaism, nor even medieval Judaism, but the

resultant of all three, modified, enriched, and challenged by two thousand years of Western civilization.

Some Christian thinkers who have penetrated to the spirit of the Jewish tradition have discovered within it resources that can enrich the content of the Christian world-view and help us meet some of the massive problems confronting the free society of the West and the international community of tomorrow. In such areas as sex, personal morality, the family, nationalism and the inter-national community, and the relationship of religious loyalty to freedom of conscience, the authentic Jewish tradition has insights and attitudes of value not only to its devotees but to all men, and particularly to its partners in the Judeo-Christian tradition.[2]

For these insights to become manifest we need a true dialogue, which is a conversation among equals. In the Middle Ages, Chris-tians talked to Jews, but it was generally a monologue, taking the form of compulsory public disputations. In these debates the Christian defender was frequently a convert from Judaism, deeply hostile to his ancestral faith and generally ignorant of its contents. Eager to display the proverbial zeal of the neophyte, he attacked Judaism with all the weapons of malice and ignorance at his dis-posal. The Jewish protagonists, on the other hand, were often re-warded with exile or other punishment for statements that could be construed as critical of Christianity.

Yet even these religious disputations, inimical as they were to true understanding, performed a signal service. They compelled the leaders of the Jewish community, which was physically and culturally segregated in the Ghetto, to examine the bases of their own faith and its relationships to its daughter religions. Here, as so often, adversity proved the mother of progress.[3]

While public religious disputations are now a thing of the past, the objective has survived into the present, albeit in slightly modified form. The effort to demonstrate the superiority of Christianity remains central to the missionary enterprise. For orthodox Christians it takes the form of presenting the so-called "proof texts" of the Old Testament, which, it is alleged, find their fulfillment in the New. The evidence is, of course, con-vincing only to those who have already accepted the belief in the central role of the Savior in the drama of human salvation. Ac-ceptance of the religious truth of the Christian dispensation is, in the last analysis, an act of faith, not subject to argument and logical demonstration.

It is here that liberal Christians, paradoxically enough, are faced with a greater problem than their more orthodox brethren.

Those who tend to accept a less literal interpretation of tradition-al Christian dogma are impelled to rest their case for the value of Christianity, not on its dogmatic content, but on its alleged ethical superiority over Judaism.

The well-worn and threadbare contrast still continues to be drawn between the Old Testament "God of justice" and the "God of love" of the New Testament. Every competent scholar, Chris-tian and Jewish alike, knows that the Old Testament conceived of God in terms of love as well as of justice, just as Jesus' God manifested Himself in justice as well as in love, for justice with-out love is cruelty, and love without justice is caprice. Neverthe-less, the practice still goes on in the pulpit and in popular publi-cations of contrasting the primitivism, tribalism, and legalism of the Old Testament with the spirituality, universalism, and freedom of the New, to the manifest disadvantage of the former.

This contrast between the Testaments is achieved by placing the lower elements of the Old Testament by the side of the higher aspects of the New, and the process is as misleading as would be the results of the opposite procedure. Thus, one of the most sympathetic and appreciative students of the New Testament, Claude G. Montefiore, writes in an eloquent passage in his « Synoptic Gospels »:

> Such passages as Matt. XXV:41 should make theologians excessively careful of drawing beloved contrasts between Old Testament and New. We find even the liberal theologian Dr. Fosdick saying: "From Sinai to Calvary--was ever a record of progressive revelation more plain or more con-vincing? The development begins with Jehovah disclosed in a thunder storm on a desert mountain, and it ends with Christ saying: 'God is a Spirit: and they that worship Him must worship in spirit and in truth'; it begins with a war-god leading his partisans to victory, and it ends with men saying 'God is love; and he that abideth in love abideth in God, and God abideth in him'; it begins with a provincial Deity, loving his tribe and hating his enemies, and it ends with the God of the whole earth worshipped by a 'great multitude, which no man could number, out of every nation and of all tribes and peoples and tongues'; it begins with a God who commands the slaying of the Amalekites, 'both man and woman, infant and suckling,'' and it ends with a Father whose will it is that 'not one of these little ones should perish'; it begins with God's people standing afar off from His light-

126

nings and praying that He might not speak to them lest they die, and it ends with men going into their chambers, and, having shut the door, praying to their Father who is in secret" (« Christianity and Progress », p. 209).

Very good. No doubt such a series can be arranged. Let me now arrange a similar series. "From Old Testament to New Testament--was ever a record of retrogression more plain or more convincing? It begins with, 'Have I any pleasure at all in the death of him that dieth, ' and it ends with, 'Begone from me, ye doers of wickedness.' It begins with, 'The Lord is slow to anger and plenteous in mercy'; it ends with 'Fear him who is able to destroy both body and soul in Gehanna.' It begins with, 'I dwell with him that is of a contrite spirit to revive it'; it ends with 'Narrow is the way which leads to life, and few there be who find it.' It begins with, 'I will not contend for ever; I will not be always wroth'; it ends with 'Depart, ye cursed, into the everlasting fire.' It begins with, 'Should not I have pity upon Nineveh, the great city?'; it ends with, 'It will be more endurable for Sodom on the day of judgment than for that city.' It begins with, 'The Lord is good to all, and near to all who call upon Him'; it ends with, 'Whosoever speaks against the Holy Spirit, there is no forgiveness for him whether in this world or the next.' It begins with, 'The Lord will wipe away tears from off all faces; he will destroy death forever'; it ends with, 'They will throw them into the furnace of fire; there is the weeping and the gnashing of teeth.'" And the one series would be as misleading as the other.[4]

Another widespread practice which should be surrendered is that of referring to the Old Testament verses quoted in the New as original New Testament passages. The Golden Rule continues to be cited from the New Testament, when the fact is that Jesus, like any Jewish teacher, was citing the Hebrew Scriptures (Matthew 22:39; Luke 10:27), as was Paul (Romans 13:9). To adduce one more instance, in an excellently written tract titled "I Believe in the Bible," published by the Congregational Christian Churches, the author contrasts the God who "orders Agag hewn to pieces before the altar" with the God "who taught through St. Paul: 'If your enemy is hungry, feed him' (Romans 12:20)." If Paul were citing chapter and verse in his labors, would he have failed to point out that he was simply quoting Proverbs 25:21 verbatim?

In sum, it would seem to one who stands outside the Christian communion, but is deeply sympathetic to its nobility and beauty and its power to lead men to greatness, that the modern teacher of Christianity, if he is to be worthy of his high calling, should have an understanding of Judaism on three principal levels: the Biblical Period, which created the Old Testament from which he draws spiritual sustenance; Normative or Rabbinic Judaism, which is the background of Jesus, the Apostles, Paul, and the early Church; and Modern Judaism, which still has its truths to speak to men and which serves as the spiritual home of several millions of his neighbors and fellow citizens.

(4) The life of the spokesman of Christianity, the Christian teacher of the twentieth century, should possess an adequate understanding of contemporary Jewry.

This last observation suggests the fourth area that should be reflected in the seminary curriculum and beyond it. Priests, ministers, and rabbis are today being brought into contact during their college and seminary training with such disciplines as politics, economics, sociology, psychology, as well as the natural sciences. It is increasingly recognized that unless the insights of religion are related to these fields, such insights will remain suspended in midair and exert no practical effect upon human conduct. The parish minister and the priest, the church administrator and the religious educator, will all serve the needs of a pluralistic society of equals more truly if they know and understand the lives and institutions, the groups and divisions, the problems and the goals, of their Jewish neighbors.

In one sense, this apparently secular approach to contemporary Jewry is of greater moment than the more theologically oriented attitudes we have previously discussed. Modern Jews are profoundly aware and deeply appreciative of the vast reservoir of goodwill to be found among Christian friends and neighbors. They know them as generally humane and compassionate, fair-minded and tolerant in their individual relationships, and allowing for the weaknesses of human nature, Jews attempt to reciprocate in kind.

However, speaking with a frankness flowing out of genuine friendship, I must confess that most Jews do not see the same virtues in evidence in the Christian community viewed as a collective entity. However paradoxical it may seem, it is almost as though men's actions were better than their professions! There is far too much evidence in the history and etiology of anti-Semitism that seems to support the view that Christian men and women display goodwill because they are human and exhibit prejudice because they are Christian.

The two major events of modern Jewish history, the Nazi holocaust and the establishment of the State of Israel, underscore the reasons for this feeling. Jews recognize that there is genuine contrition in many Christian religious circles for the horrible extermination of six million Jewish men, women, and children who were noncombatants and were cruelly done to death by Nazism. Though their emotions are deeply involved, Jews are increasingly recognizing that they must try to forgive what they cannot forget and try to forget what they cannot forgive. But the wounds are deep and the scar tissue takes time to form. Jews are also realistic enough to realize that the horrors of the crematoria and the gas chambers cannot loom as large for Christians as for Jews. They are deeply appreciative of the warm sympathy of a distinguished religious leader like Professor Wilder when he speaks of "the deep reappraisal into which all Christians must have been shocked by the mass persecutions of the recent period." The same concern underlies Father Campion's candid analysis of the varieties of ethnocentrism in our day. But Jews wonder how widely the rank and file of Christians share the sense of contrition which these and other sensitive Christians, Catholic and Protestant alike, have expressed. In the University of California survey reported on by Dr. Glock, close to half the Americans polled agreed with the statement that "Jews should stop complaining about what happened to them in Nazi Germany."

The Nazi persecution is one major event where Jews sense a less-than-adequate response from their Christian neighbors. One fervently hopes that it belongs to the past, and will never rise again. The State of Israel, which is part of the pulsating present, is another. Now it cannot be too strongly emphasized that virtually all Jews who feel any sense of attachment to their heritage are profoundly dedicated to the State of Israel as their spiritual center and the only sure refuge on earth for their oppressed brethren. If "home" may be defined as "the place they must let you in when you knock," the land of Israel is the homeland of world Jewry, in no political sense, but in spiritual terms. He who understands Judaism from within knows that the Jewish group cannot be subsumed under alien and inappropriate categories. The usual terms "religion," "nationality," or that most bloodstained of words, "race," are not applicable to the Jewish community. If truth is our goal,

Jews must be recognized as a unicum, as the Bible underscores time and again. If a description is required, Jews are a religious-cultural-ethnic group, a ponderous formula far less adequate than the short biblical term 'am, "people."[5]

When the true nature of the Jewish group and of its heritage is grasped, there is no difficulty in comprehending the relationship of Jews to the land of Israel. Everywhere in the free world, Jews are deeply committed to the lands of their sojourning and are thoroughly integrated into the political, economic, and cultural life of their native or adopted fatherlands. Nevertheless, they harbor a love for that little corner of the earth's surface where their people had its origin, where their tradition was born, where their brothers are masters of their own destiny, and where Judaism is not a minority culture. There are untold numbers of non-Jews, both within the Church and without, who have recognized the unique character of Jewish peoplehood and have been able to understand the special relationship of modern Jews to the State of Israel--a relationship which does not impugn in the slightest their loyalty to their respective countries.

To be sure, there is a tiny but highly articulate group which lives in the shadow of the bugbear of "double allegiance," which it has conjured up by its own fears and by its total estrangement from the authentic spirit of Judaism. Now this group of Jews is looked upon with profound distaste, to use no stronger word, by the vast majority of their brethren.

Since the State of Israel is not only an objective reality but an essential element in the world-view of most Jews, any true understanding of contemporary Jewry must seek to include the State of Israel. What the Jewish community would wish is not that the churches become partisans of the State of Israel or that they undertake to defend every aspect of the internal or external policy of that solitary bastion of democracy in the Middle East. Jews themselves, both in Israel and throughout the world, have not hesitated to criticize many aspects of Israeli life, and I myself am no exception. But what Jews would like to see is a growing recognition by Christians of the legitimacy of Jewish rights in Palestine, which, incidentally, does not and need not imply any denial of the legitimate rights of the Arabs. The State of Israel must be seen against the background of the massive Jewish tragedy of the twentieth century: the Nazi holocaust in the recent past, the barring of the gates against the admission of Jews in many lands of the democratic West, and their persecution in Arab lands and in the Communist East. Far too many well-intentioned members of the Christian community have yet to recognize that the State of Israel represents literally the only asylum of life and hope for untold numbers of oppressed Jews the world over.

Is it too extreme to suggest that the free world did not emerge with flying moral colors from the Nazi holocaust and that much more might have been done to minimize the Nazi murders and to save the victims? Now the State of Israel, whose existence is gravely threatened from many quarters, is another litmus paper testing the moral fiber of the Western world.

Quoting from Dr. Wilder's reference to the statement of the Bossey Consultation of the World Council of Churches in September 1956, "With respect to the State of Israel, it is stated that 'we cannot say a plain yes.' Nor can we say a plain no, 'because the church does not stand for a vague cosmopolitanism.'" One is well aware of the complex considerations that entered into this carefully balanced statement of the Bossey Consultation. But in view of the burden of guilt which lies upon the Western world, one had a right to hope that expediency would not triumph quite so completely. What should be forthcoming is not a blanket endorsement of the State of Israel, but an unequivocal statement emphasizing the historic right of the Jewish people to a homeland for its body and soul. This consideration should carry weight with Christians who cherish the Scriptures as the word of God. Dr. Chaim Weizmann was once asked at a British Royal Commission hearing what was the basis of the Jewish title to Palestine. He answered, "Gentlemen, you are under the impression that the mandate is our Bible. The truth is that the Bible is our mandate."

Undoubtedly the existence and progress of the State of Israel confronts many believing Christians with theological issues, of which I am well aware. But these difficulties should be treated as problems and not as obstacles to the expression of the moral will. The creative capacity of Christian thinkers can surely prove more than equal to the task of validating new experience by the light of age-old religious truths. The aggiornamento now taking place in the Roman Catholic Church is impressive testimony of this vitality in Christendom.

There is one more tension area which must concern all who are sincerely interested in furthering the dialogue between Christianity and Judaism. This is the long-standing tradition of missionary activity in the Christian Church. Again quoting from Dr. Wilder's reference earlier in this Conference, the traditional Christian doctrine was expressed by the International Committee on the Christian Approach to the Jews at its conference in 1931 as follows: "Judaism is as much without Christ as Mohammedan-ism and Hinduism, Buddhism and Confucianism. Either all people need Christ or none."

Jews have always been irritated by the assumption of superior-ity which underlies the widespread efforts being made to convert them to Christianity. Today this assumption is resented by other non-Christians as well, Mohammedans, Hindus, Buddhists, Con-fucianists. Each of these traditions is able to demonstrate, to the satisfaction of its own communicants at least, that it possesses adequate resources for the spiritual and ethical life of its devotees. Indeed, many of the spokesmen of non-Christian religions, survey-ing the history of the Western world during these past twenty cen-turies, are prepared to argue for the superiority of their own specific religious tradition.

Be this as it may, it is clear that the missionary goals directed to Jews vitiate the effort to establish genuine goodwill. It will be recalled that in one of the earlier drafts of the proposed schema on the Jews at the Second Vatican Council, the Christian duty of prac-ticing kindness to Jews was closely linked to the Christian hope for conversion of the Jews. It aroused a storm of protest, not only within the Jewish community, but among many leaders of the Roman Catholic Church and untold Catholic laymen, who did not abate a jot or tittle of their loyalty to their church and its teach-ing but who understood the sincerity of Jews' loyalty to Judaism.

Through the centuries, Christians have expressed their love for their fellow men by their efforts to bring them within the pale of Christian belief. Jews have been no less sincere in their love for their fellow men, but they believe that salvation is not ex-clusively of the Jews and that "the righteous of all nations have their share in the world to come." They have therefore accorded to their fellow men, by right and not merely by sufferance, in theory as well as in practice, the right to preserve their own religious tradition and group individuality.[6]

Can Christianity be asked to abandon its hope of converting Jews to the Gospel? A few Christian thinkers, among them Reinhold Niebuhr, have answered this question in the affirmative, though most Christian teachers would probably not agree. But, increasing-ly, there is a growing emphasis in Christian circles, not upon missionary activity directed toward the Jews, but, in Professor Wilder's words, upon a Christian witness to the Jews which "will take the form either of silent deeds of justice and goodness or of dialogue without ulterior motives." Christians are not called upon to abandon their hope for a world converted to the Gospels, any more than traditional Judaism has given up the Prophetic faith that the day will come when "the Lord shall be one and His name one." If the election of Israel, which is basic to the Christian claim, has any meaning, it must be that we must leave to God the achievement of His purpose through and with His people at "the end of days" and that we must express our hopes in a spirit of humility, conscious that His thoughts are not our thoughts and His ways are not our ways.

There are welcome signs of the dawning of a new day in this area. Recently a Jewish-Catholic Colloquy was held at St. Vincent's Archabbey at Latrobe, Pennsylvania, the oldest Benedictine monastery in the United States. Here, for three days, a group of Catholic and Jewish thinkers explored the relationship of their traditions and their communities. According to one published report on the Colloquy, ". . . repeated questions on the need to convert Jews were answered either that conversion is the work of God and is accomplished only by example, not by force; that the conversion of the Jews is a matter of the entire people turning to Christ, not of individuals; hence it is for the end of days and God's good time, not as a matter of the Church's immediate practical efforts. The spirit of Pope John could not have been more steadfastly and sincerely manifested."[7]

To urge a modification of attitude and practice is not as radical a proposal as may at first sight appear. The history of both Christianity and Judaism, and indeed of every living tradition, offers countless instances of doctrines as well as practices that were important at one period and then have receded into the background, sometimes to be revived at a subsequent age. In the history of Christian dogmatics, St. Paul's doctrine of justification by faith was of basic importance in his theology. That centuries later it became the central theological issue in the Reformation, separating Catholics from Protestants, is a truism of religious history. Nevertheless, Professor John Macquarrie points out that "justification" is a metaphor taken out of the lawcourts; further, he does not hesitate to say that it "has probably been given an altogether exaggerated importance in the subsequent history of Christian doctrine."[8] For the great churches of Christianity, the Second Advent has never been abandoned, but it is not central and immediate in the present hour. The Jewish tradition also exhibits many examples of ideas and practices rising and falling in importance in different eras.[9]

It should therefore be possible for Christian leadership to recognize that genuine conversion can come only through the grace of God and in His own time, and that the life of dialogue, which means talking together and living together, should not be vitiated by the hope of utilizing these contacts for missionary activities.

The Nazi holocaust, the State of Israel, and the Christian missionary tradition are the three main areas of profound concern to contemporary Jews who wish to love and respect their brothers and hope to be respected and loved by them. The religious teachers of tomorrow, who are being trained in the seminaries of today, need to be led to a sympathetic understanding of Jewish attitudes and feelings on these crucial subjects.

According to Hasidic tradition, the great saint Rabbi Levi Yitzohak of Berditchev was wont to say that he had learned the meaning of love from an ignorant peasant. One day he had occasion to come into an inn, in the corner of which two peasants were sitting over their liquor, far gone "in their cups." They were at the sentimental stage, throwing their arms around one another and telling how much they loved each other. Suddenly the one turned to his companion and said, "Ivan, what hurts me now?" Ivan answered, "Peter, how should I know what hurts you?" Whereupon Ivan answered, "If you do not know what hurts me, how can you say you love me?" This, said the Rabbi, is the truest definition of love.

In suggesting that the Christian seminary should include Judaism in its curriculum for the training of priests and ministers, I am urging more than an occasional interfaith meeting or invitation to a guest speaker, valuable as these person-to-person contacts are. The basic need is for systematic teaching of the salient aspects of Judaism by competent scholars.

This proposal is neither impractical nor utopian, given the conviction that we who are dedicated to religion must set our own house in order before we venture to convert the world. As a member of a seminary faculty I am fully aware of the pressures upon the curriculum from many quarters and the difficulty of adding new courses for the student. Nor have I overlooked the fact that most seminary students are not preparing to be scholars and that only a mere handful of those who are may want to be specialists on Judaism.

What would be required to implement the program set forth here? It seems to me that only two basic courses need to be added to the seminary cirriculum. One would deal with the "History of Judaism" and would trace the history of the Jewish religion from its inception through the rabbinic and medieval periods to the modern age. The student would thus achieve a knowledge of his-torical Judaism and an understanding of contemporary Jews and Judaism. The second course on "The Ideas and Practices of Judaism" would set forth the basic religious doctrines of Judaism, its ethical teaching and its ritual system. On the basis of a decade of experience in teaching at Columbia University, I have no hesi-tation in saying that each of these courses could be presented in a two-hour session for one year.

The classical sources of Judaism are increasingly available in English in authoritative and accessible form. Interesting and fair-minded presentations of the content and history of Judaism are constantly appearing. It seems to me entirely feasible for Christian seminaries to follow the pioneering practice of several divinity schools by adding a scholar on Judaism to their faculties. This has become a widespread practice in many secular colleges and universities that are offering such courses to their students, who are laymen. The seminaries, I submit, should do no less.

The effort and sacrifice required to introduce such a program into the Christian seminary curriculum will perhaps be easier to muster if we remember that the benefits will go far beyond a growth in intergroup understanding, however desirable, indeed essential, this is. Each religion possesses profound insights which are of great value, though not free from weaknesses; each tradition can prove salutary to the other because of its varied content and emphasis. In his brief but stimulating paper, Pro-fessor Joseph Sittler has highlighted several such instances. We add a few more from another perspective.

The tradition of Judaism is fundamentally life-affirming. It sees in the phenomena of the natural world the abundant signs of the presence of the Living God. Yet the enjoyment of life's pleasures can easily be distorted into hedonism and material-ism, and degenerate into license and irresponsibility. Here the correctives of discipline and of asceticism are needed to em-phasize the virtues of self-restraint and moderation and to stress the limited significance of the material aspect of existence. Such a counterbalance is to be found in the ascetic tendencies which exist in all religions to some degree, but which are stronger in classical Christianity than in Judaism.

From the days of St. Paul, Christianity has underscored the truth that "the letter killeth, but the spirit giveth life" (II Corin-thians 3:6). Yet always there is the grave danger of a vague spirituality spending itself in emotion, but finding no concrete manifestation in life. Here the emphasis upon works and not

135

merely upon faith, which characterizes Judaism, is a valuable corrective. The stress upon conduct embodied in law, which Judaism has exemplified through the ages through the development of the Halakah, is today increasingly recognized as an essential ingredient of a perdurable society.

Judaism is a faith intimately linked to an ethnic group, though its universalistic vision encompasses all men. Christianity takes pride in knowing no ethnic boundaries, but it sets up standards of belief as essential to salvation. Christianity can help safeguard Judaism against weakening its universalistic aspect. Judaism can remind Christianity that national loyalty is neither irrelevant nor hostile to the good life and that granting freedom of religion to those who differ with us is entirely compatible with a strong commitment to one's own faith.

The Christian doctrine of original sin, particularly as reinterpreted by some contemporary thinkers, has already influenced the thought of several modern exponents of Judaism. It has served to reveal the dark depths within the human soul which an easy and superficial optimism has tended to overlook. Traditional Judaism, on the other hand, takes a realistic view of human nature, without accepting the doctrine of original sin. From its vantage point it is able to offer guidelines for dealing with such agonizing problems as personal and family morality, race relations, religious differences and national loyalties within the context of a world community.

The dialogue between the two faiths might well address itself to such themes as the tension between law and freedom, the different values of the ethics of self-fulfillment and of self-abnegation,[10] the relationship of the material and the spiritual, the dichotomy between the letter and the spirit, the role of ethnic loyalty in the world community, the nature of man and his impulses--issues with regard to which there is a difference in content or emphasis in Judaism and in Christianity.

To one Jewish observer, at least, there seems to be evidence that contemporary Christianity is moving toward a greater appreciation of attitudes and insights that have always been congenial to Judaism. The new emphasis in Catholic circles on the principle of collegiality and the role of the laity as the people of God, the reconsideration of the functions of marriage, the modification of ascetic practices, and the growing involvement of the religious in the problems of the secular world, these are all reactions characteristic of Normative Judaism. The search for new formulations of Christian doctrine and practice associated with such thinkers as John Courtney Murray and Hans Küng, Paul Tillich and Reinhold Niebuhr, and with such churchmen as Bishop Robinson in England and Bishop Pike in America, have naturally aroused vigorous and conflicting reactions. But it is such differences that are the stuff of meaningful dialogue, making for the revitalization of religious truth.

Conducted on the basis of knowledge and mutual respect, dialogue between the two components of the Judeo-Christian tradition can prove a blessing to both and a beacon to our age. By including a study of Judaism and the Jewish people in the curriculum, Christian seminaries can prepare the religious teachers of tomorrow to serve God and His cause. In the words of an ancient sage, "The world stands upon three pillars: upon truth, upon justice and upon peace. And all three are one. For where truth is cherished and justice prevails, peace is established."[11] In seeking to speak the truth for the sake of justice we shall help to advance the reign of God's kingdom on earth, the hallmark of which is peace.

1 For an elaboration of these conclusions, see the writer's "The Significance of the Dead Sea Scrolls," in Jewish Frontier, April 1957, pp. 17-24.

2 The writer has sought to expound some of these viable and significant elements of the Jewish tradition in Judaism for the Modern Age (New York, 1955) and The Root and the Branch: Judaism and the Free Society (Chicago, 1962).

3 See the excellent and balanced study of S. Katz, Exclusivism and Tolerance (Oxford, 1961).

4 Claude G. Montefiore, Synoptic Gospels (London, 1909), vol. II, p. 326.

5 For a detailed discussion of the nature of the Jewish group identity and the conclusion set forth in our text, see Judaism for the Modern Age, pp. 19-48, and The Root and the Branch, pp. 19-30.

6 For a presentation of the attitudes of traditional Judaism to other faiths, see The Root and the Branch, pp. 42-53.

7 Rabbi Eugene B. Borowitz, "A Jewish-Catholic Colloquy," in Congress Weekly, March 1965, pp. 7-8.

8 In his review of Hans Küng's new book, Justification: The Doctrine of Karl Barth and a Catholic Reflection, in New York Times Book Review, March 7, 1965, p. 18.

9 See "The Nature of Jewish Tradition" and "Tradition and Growth and Development, " in Judaism for the Modern Age, pp. 127-52, 166-85.

10 On these categories, see the writer's Politics and Ethics (Santa Barbara, Cal., 1961) and The Root and the Branch, chs. IX, X.

11 Jerusalem Talmud, Taanit 4, 5.

SEVENTEEN

Summary and conclusion

J. Bruce Long

The Conference from which this volume springs was not intended
to be merely a general dialogue between Jews and Christians, but
rather a concerted analysis by and discussion among Christians--
Roman Catholic and Protestant--of Christian theological training
in relationship to its treatment of Judaism. A Jewish organization,
the Anti-Defamation League of B'nai B'rith, prompted a representative group of Christian theological educators to undertake a
critical evaluation of one facet of Christian teaching as related to
Jews and the Jewish faith. In addition to instigating the discussion,
this organization provided additional evidence of the persistence
of anti-Semitic attitudes in America as exhibited by social and
economic discrimination on the secular scene and by stereotyped
notions entertained by Christians about the "curse" that rests upon
Jews for the death of Jesus.

An account of the history of the Conference calls for two preliminary observations. First of all, let it be said that the very fact a Jewish organization felt free to invite Christian theological educators to convoke a gathering such as this bears telling witness to the freedom and self-assurance that is a novel aspect of Jewish experience in the American scene. It is, of course, fitting and proper that Christians should be challenged to examine their tradition in terms of the attitudes of Jews and Judaism. But what is perhaps unique to the American experience is that here Jews should feel free to issue such a challenge without experiencing fear or embarrassment. For centuries Jewish existence depended upon the parsimonious sufferance of Christians. In asking Christians to call this Conference, the Jew was, in fact, assuming his existence as a matter of inherent right. The Conference reflects an entirely new view of Jewish-Christian relations in which both traditions are seeking respect and understanding. For this both Christians and Jews can be thankful.

There is a second observation which pertains to the calling of this Conference, that is, the changing character of the relations between the two Christian communities. After more than four hundred years of separation there is evidence today that the effort to achieve a more honest exchange of ideas and impressions across the gulf that separates divided brethren is in process. The conducted tours we give each other through our respective domains are increasingly thorough and realistic. We have begun to share with one another our doubts and problems as well as our certainties and achievements. But we have only begun. And a critical analysis of our respective systems of theological education in each other's presence, so to speak, is a somewhat novel and most encouraging event, at least in the United States. The Anti-Defamation League introduced a new note of frankness into the ecumenical dialogue between Catholics and Protestants when it persuaded them to hold this Conference on the treatment of Jews and the Jewish faith in Christian theological training. That this was seemingly done unwittingly or inadvertently is a fact which enhances the authenticity of the act. Moreover, it seems entirely fitting that separated Christians should thus concentrate on a common attitude, namely, their attitude toward Judaism. There was no conflict about this matter among Christians when they separated four centuries ago, and at least until very recently Romans and non-Romans alike have cut the same figure in their teaching about the role and fate of the Jew in the Divine Plan-- past, present, and future. If there is any relevant issue which all Western Christians can discuss without having to fight the Reformation over again, it is this one. In this matter the sin and the guilt are the same for all Christians; and the repentance and grace of forgiveness that have never failed to follow in their wake, however belatedly, are similarly a common experience and part of a common history for both Protestant and Roman Christians.

It is clear, from every point of view, that this Conference was a pioneering venture. It is an achievement of some magnitude that a conference such as this took place at all. The failures and errors of judgment must be laid to its pioneering character, not to the incompetency of either the organizers or participants. Like all similar ventures, the initial thrust was cautious and halting, and the immediate results are "preliminary." It is, however, a most significant initial effort by Protestants and Catholics to discuss, analyze, and evaluate their respective understandings of Judaism as an historic faith and the ways in which the thought and literature of this tradition are being taught to present-day seminarians. Hopefully, this pioneering venture will provoke further conferences of like nature where the problems and issues treated here in a partial and preliminary manner will be probed at greater depth.

The substance of the Conference--the ideas, impressions, and insights gained from the papers and the discussion sessions-- might be thrown into bold relief by merely presenting a few of the most salient ideas that emerged in the course of the meeting.

(1) Professor William D. Davies indicated concern that the Church had severed its ties with the Synagogue tradition as embodied in normative Judaism and had thereby impoverished its moral and religious life. To quote Davies: "Where the Jewish rootage of Christianity is neglected, the Church tends to lose awareness of the Living God at work in history in favor of other-worldliness, mysticism and gnosis; it tends to lessen the astringent moral imperative of the call to live out its faith in the world; it tends to lose awareness of itself as above all a people, and not a structured organization, and to forsake the world for the wrong reasons."

In the discussion following Dr. Davies' presentation, Dr. J. Coert Rylaarsdam contested Davies' claim that the otherworldliness in Christianity was brought about by neglect of the legacy of the Synagogue. He contended, to the contrary, that the cause is to be found centered inherently in the nature of the eschatological community itself. Dr. Rylaarsdam continued: "The greatest damage to the Christian tradition was done by the processes of Hellenization and Romanization. It was by means of the corrosive effects of these two processes that the Church lost the awareness of what the Old Testament means by 'living God.' The term 'monotheism' is at best an ambiguous term in the Christian tradition and always has been. It is not a biblical word, but came into wide usage in the fourth century as a static term to designate the action of God in Christ. A strong Christocentrism grew out of that static inter- pretation of God's presence in the world. For this reason Jews have always found it difficult to understand the rationale of Chris- tian theology that is either radically Christocentric or Trinitarian. This is a problem that grows out of the quasi-philosophical character of the phrasing of our symbols of the faith rather than out of any fundamental divergence between the two faiths."

Dr. Davies agreed with this point, but added that "by and large, the Church has failed to make the eschatological dimension of faith relevant to life in this world precisely by neglecting the legal tradition of Judaism. For the Jew the Law is the 'mint of prophecy,' the acid test of loyalty to God's commandments; and we Christians, especially Protestants, have traditionally been extremely suspicious of the Law. Thus a broad gap has developed between the eschatologica' demands of the Gospel and the actual demands of society upon us."

Father Dennis J. McCarthy, S.J. (Associate Professor of Sacred Scripture, St. Mary's College Divinity School, St. Marys, Kansas), took issue with both the previous speakers by denying that the break with Judaism hindered the Church from involving herself in the "mud of history." He asserted, instead, that the otherworldliness in the Church began to become visible only in the fifteenth century, after the Council of Trent; it was then--and not before, as Dr. Davies contended--that the break with the world became so definite.

Dr. Rylaarsdam retorted by observing that "whenever the Church had been in the world from the fifth century onward, it had been there for the sake of getting out of the world--that is, the essential task of the Church has been to realize the end which lies beyond the world, not one that is embodied in the world of time and space. In short, the business of the Christian's life in the world is to attain the state of grace, to accumulate that grace in one way or another, so that he will stand in good stead in the world to come. It is here that both factions of Christianity stand over against Judaism, be- cause for the latter the 'mud of history' is where God began his work in the world and it is here that he will bring that work to consummation."

As the Conference progressed, a consensus materialized among the conferees that additional provisions must be made to hasten and guarantee the authenticity of the ecumenical endeavor, to open avenues of interchange between Jews and Christians. The Jew and the Christian have much to learn from one another. As Professor Rylaarsdam noted in the first discussion: "From the Jew the Christian can learn of the effectiveness of the Word of God in working out the salvation of man in history. From the Christian the Jew must discover that God's revelation is not constricted by or restricted to the historical forms of the Jewish faith, but arises in forms alien to the expectations of men."

One corrective to the hostility between the Christian and Jewish communities which has been expressed in so many heinous forms during the past one hundred years is to recover, as fully as possible, that common heritage which has informed and shaped both traditions. Indeed, the recognition of this shared tradition might do much to remedy the insensitivity on the part of Christians to the legitimate existence and mission of Judaism. Hopefully, a renewed mutual recognition of this common history by both groups might issue into an attitude that would reach out beyond mere tolerance to a more creative relationship based on mutual acceptance.

(2) Increased attention should be given to Judaism as an historical phenomenon, that is, as a growing, developing, evolving historical organism. Judaism, like Christianity (or any other social institution for that matter), is not a static sociological group planted at a single point in history without phases of life, death, and alteration. It is a sociohistorical organism which constantly exhibits changing nuances of life, faith, and thought. Indeed, we might go so far as to say that one of the primary factors in the lack of understanding of Judaism by modern Christians is that the latter tend to restrict their image of Judaism to its classical formulation in the Old Testament. Even that provincial vision of Judaism is often further restricted to the prophetic movements. The extension of the Christian vision of Judaism to include its rabbinic, medieval, and modern reformed expressions would do much to alleviate the common cause of this misunderstanding.

A natural corollary to this idea is that both religious traditions, if there is to be any significant and effectual degree of understanding between them, must recover an awareness of the complexity, the multifarious character of each tradition.

(3) During one of the discussions Rabbi Monford Harris (Associate Professor of Religious Philosophy, College of Jewish

Studies, Chicago) observed that there is a novel and somewhat disturbing force at work in American culture which is coloring the whole fabric of religious life and is affecting the development of religion, not only within each respective religious community, but among the representative groups. "We must consider the situation of the contemporary American Jew in this connection," Rabbi Harris contended. "What is haunting us here is that, historically, Jews are in a different situation today in America than are most representatives of the Christian community--that is, the Jew, since the seventeenth century, has been involved in a remarkably revolutionary change vis-à-vis the modern secular world. The Jews, particularly in America, have been wrenched out of the tradition-bound world which was their natural heritage in Europe. As a result, it is becoming increasingly difficult to point to a representative pattern of Jewish life today, to a paradigm to which the modern Jew can conform. I have grave doubts about the modern Jew's preparation for the kind of dialogue that is being forced upon him by historical circumstances because of the depth and extensiveness of this involvement in secularism today. Secularism has become widespread in the Jewish community only during the past fifty to seventy-five years. The European Jewish community life was one wholly committed to Jewish faith and piety in all its reaches and levels. Given the fact that secularism is crowding in upon both Jewish and Christian life, the basic point of departure for Jewish-Christian dialogue is not those affirmations that we hold in common, but the recognition of a common cross which is the creation of secularism."

(4) Father Donald R. Campion, S.J., raised what is perhaps the central issue in the whole matter of Jewish-Christian relations, and one which inevitably plays a central role in any discussion of the interrelationship between the two religious groups. Namely, does ethnocentrism--cultural, ethnic, or religious--necessarily produce negative or belligerent attitudes toward members of other religious groups? Is it possible for one to be loyal to his own religious tradition without exercising a hostile attitude toward the "other" who is present in the person of the unbeliever or the theological outsider? As Campion stated the matter, "each of the major traditions cherishes among its most fundamental tenets a set of absolutes which are at odds with the bigotry we associate with the ethnocentric personality." Therefore, an authentic religious faith, one which grows out of a deep internalization of the moral and religious precepts of a religious tradition, need not necessarily create or nourish bitter attitudes

toward members of other religious groups. On the contrary, the more firmly committed a person is to the religious imperatives of his faith, the more open to and tolerant of the religious "outsider" he should become.

Father Campion also stated: "It is one thing to insist, as I do, that ethnocentrism, is at root a 'neutral' concept, and that Christian ethnocentrism, specifically, need not issue in prejudice, hostility or contempt toward non-Christians, and in particular, Jews. It is another to recognize clearly and without cavil that Christian ethnocentrism has assumed hideous forms and can prove to be a climate for anti-Semitism." Our task is "to inquire how such things could happen and to discuss means of preventing their recurrence."

(5) The question of prime importance is this: How can a Christian believer affirm Judaism as a living and viable faith while at the same time remaining loyal to his own commitment? Is there room in Christian theology for the affirmation of the legitimacy of the other? Or is the case as André Gide recorded it in his personal journal: "The difficulty comes from this, that Christinity [Christian orthodoxy] is exclusive and that belief in its truth excludes belief in any other truth. It does not absorb; it excludes."?

The judgment of this issue as to what degree the Christian Church has been open and receptive to members of other faiths was not rendered conclusively in either the positive or negative mode. But Dr. Amos N. Wilder remarked, "There is undoubtedly a belated anti-Semitism which infects Christianity, and that attitude is perhaps motivated primarily by the belief that Jews will not be saved. The belief that Christ has provided the ultimate salvation of all mankind is inherent in one's loyalty to the Christian message; that much is true. But it is a question of what motivates a man to believe Christ to be the Savior of the world. Is the belief held in a spirit of self-justification and self-aggrandizement or in a spirit of humility and charity toward nonbelievers? It seems to me that the former spirit has dominated over the latter, and if so, this is a great and tragic failure of the Church."

(6) Perhaps what was the most beneficial discovery of the Conference was the public verification of Josiah Royce's theory that there is such a thing as "community of interpretation." That is, only in dialogue do we complete our thought. Without the benefit of the mutual interchange of contrary points of view, ideas, and attitudes, one's thought, even at best, is partial and inaccurate. Without dialogue, genuine thought is impossible; furthermore,

dialogue begins with the recognition of a lack, a vacuum, in the point of view of each party involved. Thus authentic and creative dialogue is not simply a means by which one informs others of his own opinions, but rather a way by which one's own ideas and attitudes--and, ultimately one's own judgments--are formed and completed.

(7) The question was raised at numerous points during the Conference as to whether the term "ecumenism," both as a concept and as a working principle, has not been defined in a narrow inter-Christian way, excluding entirely the role which the Jews might play in a broader, more truly ecumenical endeavor. Should not our definition of ecumenism be expanded to include Judaism? If so, how can this be done without endangering the integrity and coherence of the Protestant-Catholic movement now underway? On the other hand, would not the integrity of the Christian ecumenical endeavor be considerably enhanced by a more encompassing definition of ecumenism? We suggest that this cannot be done until Christians are willing to give Jews a rightful place in the scheme of things. The question remains for the Christian Church to decide all over again: Is the Law superseded in the coming of Christ; has the Old Israel any longer a raison d'être now that the New Israel has come? Finally, if the New does not blot out and obliterate the effectiveness of the Old, but fulfills it, as Professor Davies contends, what do Christians mean by saying "the New fulfills the Old"?

(8) There are two main causes of anti-Semitic attitudes and actions which correlate directly with the two major types of anti-Semitism. On the one hand, there is what Samuel Sandmel has called "axiomatic anti-Semitism," which is a natural, necessary, given, theological anti-Semitism (or, more properly, anti-Judaism). This type grows naturally out of one's commitment and witness to a particular religious faith. According to Professor Wilder, it evolves inevitably from religious particularism. He believes that there is in Christianity "a particularism which nurtures the attitude that all Jews are going to be damned because of their rejection of Jesus Christ as the Chosen One of God" and that "Christianity seems to carry within itself a built-in sense of security and self-justification with respect to the salvation of the world." Father Campion, quoting Allport, contends to the contrary that an authentic, deeply internalized religious faith provokes less prejudice toward adherents of other religious faiths than a more external and institutional commitment. The question as to which of the interpretations is more correct must be left to future debate. The second type of anti-

Semitism was variously labeled as unnatural, unnecessary, ethnic-cultural, nontheological. This attitude is provoked and nurtured by an uncertainty as to the sanctity and security of one's own religious faith and is expressed in acts of hostility, resentment, and even violence, toward members of the other tradition.

Rabbi Ralph Simon (Congregation Rodfei Zedek, Chicago) pushed the thinking of the conferees out beyond this simple distinction between positive and negative anti-Semitism by alerting the group to analogous distinctions in attitudes among Jews, namely, "anti-Gentilism" and "anti-Christianism." The former attitude is a natural outgrowth of the disastrous events in recent Jewish history. From continued experiences of rejection and persecution the Jews have built up many necessary inner defenses, which, when allowed to fester, degenerate into hatred and resentment. The problem of anti-Christian attitudes, Simon contended, is more profound and crucial than the first one, for this problem is directly related to the deep suspicions which many Jews have toward Christian-Jewish dialogues per se. He made mention of the fact that "there is a long history of involuntary Jewish-Christian dialogues which stretch back into the Middle Ages, when such encounters were called 'disputations.' We recall, for example, that Nachmanides of Spain was brought by royal command to participate in a disputation with a representative of the Christian persuasion. Following the disputation, he was forced to pack up and flee for his life. Why was this? There existed in the minds of the Christians a feeling that if the Jew were confronted with the truth of the Christian message, he would accept it without hesitation. It was only a question of telling him the truth; and once he had seen it clearly, there was no doubt but that he would convert. The failure of the Jew to be persuaded by the disputation aroused deep resentment."

Returning to a consideration of present-day interreligious dialogues, Rabbi Simon said, "These discussions, I sometimes feel, do more to add fuel to the fire than to provide water to extinguish it. It is important for the Jew to know that he has been invited to these sessions to teach and to learn. But the Christian must understand that to participate in a dialogue with his Jewish friends does not give him the license to pressure the Jew into conversion. It must be clear that the Jew's openness to discussion does not mean that he is on the verge of entering the Church. We are not Christians, nor are we candidates for conversion."

(9) Dr. Charles Y. Glock, reporting on an extensive study of the variety of expressions of anti-Semitism in America and their

causes, stated that his working-theory that "any remnant of a connection between Christian beliefs and anti-Semitism would be the result of a persistence among Christians to hold to a rigidly orthodox faith and to do so in what we have called 'particularistic' terms" had been confirmed. The final results of this survey and of Dr. Glock's paper may best be summarized by listing the five links making up the causal chain leading from Christian beliefs to secular anti-Semitism, as analyzed in this study. The first link is an intimate causal relation between Christian orthodoxy and Christian particularism, whereby a Christian believer holds the message of Christ and his Church to be not only true but the only true way to salvation. This particularistic belief in the ultimacy of the Christian message is bound to provoke a deeply felt desire to convert the "apostates" to the one true faith. Next, once this summons to conversion is rejected, the hostility latent in the heart of the Christian is likely to be activated. Third, the extremely provocative missionary zeal felt by particularistic Christians and the hostility generated by rejection of the one true faith are most likely to be directed toward the Jews as a body for the simple reason that it is the largest and most prominent body of religious "outsiders" in America. Fourth, this hostility toward the Jews is motivated, by and large, by a belief that all Jews, both historical and contemporary, are responsible for the crucifixion of Jesus. Those Christians most notably associated with particularism maintain that the Jews have remained guilty and are condemned under the wrath of God for all time. The condemnation thus accrued by the Jews in killing the Son of God would be atoned for only as they accepted salvation through Christ. Finally, this religious hostility tends, in most cases, to perpetuate itself in the form of "secular anti-Semitism" by accepting negative stereotypes of Jews and by evaluating them on other than purely religious grounds. The results of the study showed that not all the factors appeared in every instance, nor did they necessarily appear in this sequence. But Dr. Glock's survey did show that a major number of the cases studied did manifest anti-Semitic sentiments, either religious or secular, and that even anti-Semitic attitudes of the secular type originated from more seminal "religious" reasons.

(10) This discovery of the role played by religious particularism in the dissemination of anti-Semitism, both religious and secular, led naturally to the question of the relative merits of particularism itself. There emerged a relative degree of consensus from the statements of Dr. Glock, Rabbi Harris, Professor Wilder, and

Rabbi Robert Gordis to the effect that the problem of religious pluralism in America is not what is the best means to rid ourselves of the last vestige of religious and cultural particularity, but rather how can we preserve the character of our various particularities while allowing for the free expression of other particularities. The problem is of such complexity and enormity that it cannot be dealt with by making the simple-minded equation "particularism versus universalism," as some sociologists have done. If we give up our own particularity for the sake of some more "desirable" universalism, we risk sacrificing all links of personal institutional identity. We end up, in the words of Rabbi Harris, "with some brand of gnosticism," each individual forsaken by the community to discover for himself whatever parts of divinity he may possess within his own soul.

Furthermore, there was a consensus among the conferees that the resources of religious pluralism must not be sought in the signal creeds and dogmas of American life. The sources must rather be sought in the religious affirmations which Christians and Jews make within their own covenants. If we attempt to solve the problem of pluralism by appealing to the Declaration of Independence or the Constitution, then we are absolutizing American experience, making it normative for all religious claims. Such an act, indeed, smacks of idolatry for the Jew as well as the Christian. The difficulty of allowing a degree of legitimacy to a religion other than one's own can be lessened as one recognizes that the desire to convert nonbelievers to his own persuasion, in its best aspects, arises out of a profound commitment to his own faith and a deep concern for the salvation of his fellowmen. This is true for both Jews and Christians. The congruence of these motivations of both religious groups--which spring from a single source, that is, love for fellowman and concern for his general welfare--may bring the Jew and Christian alike to recognize the necessity for religious pluralism. But, as both Harris and Gordis cautioned, this adoption of religious pluralism as a way of life must not be accepted merely as a fact of American life, but as an essential expression of "the Divine Love for variety."

(11) If future confrontations between Jewish and Christian bodies in conferences such as this are to be anything more than enjoyable exchanges of personal points of view, if indeed we are to have dialogue rather than harmless discussion or entertaining debate, we must face one another with an awareness that the other possesses something we lack and that creative dialogue is the first step toward remedying that lack. According to Father Dominic

M. Crossman, O.S.M. (Professor of Scripture, Stonebridge Priory, Lake Bluff, Illinois), "The great overriding lack in the Christian Church resulted from the Church's act of cutting itself free from its Judaic roots. As a consequence, the Christian Church has lost the ability to bring the eschatological Kingdom of God down into the 'mud of history'--and this in spite of the fact that both the Old Testament Prophets and Jesus were so firmly committed to the needs of men and the demands of justice. If the dialogue with the Jewish community is to bear any lasting fruits, the Church must once again regain possession of its roots in history and in its Judaic past."

(12) The most important prelude to any Jewish-Christian dialogue is for Christians to grant to Judaism a degree of legitimacy and, thereby, to dispel the Jew's fear that the invitation to dialogue is nothing more than an invitation to conversion in dialogic garb. Dr. Rylaarsdam defined the term "legitimacy" as the "recognition by the Christian that the presence of the Christian in covenant with God does not abrogate the covenant of Israel with God." And he continued, "No matter how sincerely and kindly the Christian may use such terms as 'completion' or 'filfillment' to describe the relationship of Christianity to Judaism, such words call forth all kinds of anxieties, resentments, and denials in the Jewish breast. If such terms are interpreted in a traditional fashion, it means that there is nothing for the Jew to do; he no longer has a role to play in actualizing God's covenant with his people--he is, so to speak, religiously out of business. . . . There is still in the minds of devout and committed Jews a remnant of fear that the supposed religious dialogue with their Christian neighbors is, in point of fact, a Christian monologue. As to the question of Jews taking the lead in initiating dialogues with their Christian neighbors, Christians must learn that sometimes the Jewish initiative is a mark of hope and anticipation mixed with the insecurity and uncertainty that continue to haunt Jewish life even in modern America." Campaigns for the conversion of Jews are a subtle form of threat raising the question of the theological and historical legitimacy of the Jews, and it is only upon assured respect for this legitimacy that real dialogue can be based.

Rabbi Solomon Bernards (Anti-Defamation League of B'nai B'rith) emphasized that "Jews, in their relationship to Christians, are not interested only in de facto recognition but also in de jure recognition." He continued, "The Jewish people must feel free to live out their destiny in complete acceptance by their Jewish and

Christian neighbors, and to do so without feeling that they are theologically and socially objectionable to their fellowmen. The real problem confronting this Conference is that if there is to be an extension of the interchange of ideas, values, and interpretations at the lay level of the Jewish and Christian communities, a deep sense of mutual trust and respect must first develop among the thoughtful leaders of both communities."

(13) The general issue around which the oral presentations and discussions were centered is best expressed in the title of the conference, "Judaism and the Christian Seminary Curriculum." While most of the proceedings were directed toward those broad and subtle factors in seminary training which form a landscape for the central problem of Jewish-Christian relations, on a number of occasions the conferees spoke directly to the more specific problems. Father William G. Topmoeller, S.J. (Professor of Systematic and Ecumenical Theology, St. Mary of the Lake Seminary, Mundelein, Illinois), suggested that in order to implement the "new insights into the mission and message of the Church" gained from increased personal and institutional contact between Christians and Jews and to carry out certain revisions in seminary curriculum and methods of instruction demanded by these new perspectives, "we might do well to emphasize the practical and procedural factors." Father Topmoeller specifically suggested that Christian seminaries might begin to close the gap of understanding between Christian and Jewish seminaries by "inviting guest professors, initiating dialogues among students of the three religious communities . . . and by whatever other means might be devised and discovered to break down some of the barriers of mutual understanding."

Professor Joseph Sittler countered these suggestions with the observation that "to invite a Jewish professor or scholar to teach for a semester or a year in a Christian seminary might cause a rattling of the procedural machinery that would be difficult to accommodate in some seminaries and would not be possible in others. At any rate, the task of effectively creating an interreligious exchange of this type must begin by a change in attitude and point of view within the instructors themselves. It is not by encountering a Jewish theologian for a brief exchange of views that creates a common sympathy between us, but a continual interaction with Jews in their own world. Reading stories out of the Jewish tradition, for instance, has set up within me a sense for a certain form of reality as expressed in these religious and folk stories. To the extent that I feel these people's feelings and share in their ambitions

151

and anxieties--in a word, to the degree that I can enter their world by vicarious participation in their literature--the story of their life becomes the story of my life at the level of our common human-ity. Such interchanges of understanding will come naturally out of each person's participation in the world of another. To invent pro-cedures by which men can overcome centuries-old barriers as a means of arriving at a point of mutual understanding is no longer necessary. Whatever procedure is selected is suddenly and un-expectedly changed from the inside."

Professor Rylaarsdam elaborated this point of view by observing that "whatever alterations do take place in our attitudes toward other religious communities occur by means of the total education process. Merely inviting a guest professor to offer a series of lectures concerning some topic in his own area of specialization will do little to change the status quo. After all, we have had visiting professors at the University of Chicago who left behind nothing more than slight traces of their presence. Unless the professors and students themselves come to grips with the issues which arise from an encounter between conflicting points of view--whatever these issues happen to be: Church-State re-lations in America, the Church and race relations, the Jewish-Christian dialogue, and so forth--the problems and dilemmas at hand will remain largely unaltered."

Thus the consensus of the conferees seemed to be that while certain definite and concrete changes in both course offerings and methods of teaching in the Christian seminary are called for, these innovations on the practical level will bring forth creative and lasting results only if they emerge from and are nurtured by a more general change in the climate of opinions between the Christian and Jewish communities. A totally new philosophy of education may be called for--a new approach to theological edu-cation in which the Christian seminaries claim for themselves a more appreciative understanding of the contemporary as well as the classical form of Judaism.

The Conference repeatedly hinted at the fact that the New Testament is a partisan book insofar as it is a human and his-torical book--that is, as it was influenced by the social, political, religious, and philosophical climate out of which it arose. It is a book full of echoes of the conflict between Judaism and the nascent Christian community. It is a book in which the Church seeks to justify its separation from the Synagogue; and since it was written by zealous partisans, it does not find it pos-sible to be entirely "fair" to its opponents. The enhancement of the revelation and experience it exalts is achieved, at least in part, by depreciating the legacy it "fulfills" or "displaces" or by calling into question the sincerity of those who remain faithful to it. This fact, however, was only hinted at during the course of the Conference. It was not explored, analyzed, or documented in detail; nor, for that matter, was it faced up to with full frankness. Considering the novelty of the occasion and the enterprise, this was probably inevitable. But the fact must not be left unnoticed in this concluding statement. We are dealing with issues whose "lines" were set almost two thousand years ago. Only patient and persistent attention to the problems and issues involved will enable us to reactivate the real questions, to discriminate between the transient and the enduring, and thereby to set ourselves free from crippling stereotypes mellifluously perpetuated through the centuries. We must recover a real awareness of the fact that in what it says about Jews and Judaism, the New Testament is a time-conditioned document, not a dogmatic treatise. The Conference reminded us that this is a "must," but it did not achieve that realization fully.

Only when Christians become more acutely aware that the question of the relation between Israel and the Church had not been decided when the canon of the New Testament was defined will the basis be laid for dialogue between Jew and Christian. Indeed, if one takes an historical view of religious development, he cannot deny that the Church's understanding of its relation to Israel has at various times undergone change. Christians today may still continue to develop new insights in order to account for the somewhat novel factors which determine their relationship to Jews. The issue is not that the Church has not decided its theology, either in the first century or the twentieth, but rather that the Church at this moment, as in other moments in history, is engaged in an effort to reassess and reevaluate its theology in the light of new elements. Perpetuating the normative Christian position with respect to the Jews permits no dialogue, whether the position takes a benign or vindictive mood, whether it talks about Christianity as the "fulfillment" of Judaism or about the "curse" of God upon the Jews. If the New Covenant makes the Old superfluous, whether by displacement or by absorption, there is no room for discussion between Christian and Jew. The Christian suspects the Jew of being under a ghetto mentality, theologically speaking. But the Jew, on his part, is in despair over Christian "arrogance." How can one engage in dialogue when there is nothing left to talk about?

Regardless of the degree to which one accepts or rejects the traditional assumptions of Christian theology regarding the "continuity" or the "demise" of Judaism with the birth of Christianity, it seems clear that these perspectives have led to a point of impasse. The problems raised by the anti-Semitic outbursts in Europe during the past century and in America within the past decade have emphasized the need to review and reexamine the traditional Christian view of the Jewish community. What is desperately needed at this time is a new vision on the part of Christians in their relationship to Jews, both theologically and sociologically--a vision which would force us out beyond the present impasse and would permit us to define the problem in terms less tangential to a solution. In other words, we need to bring into focus radically new analytic and interpretative perspectives. To face the issue and solve the dilemma, we need to find ways that will point up theological and sociological alternatives to the hidebound views which have not been adequate to the demands of the situation.

The search for alternatives must begin initially with the raising of certain basic methodological questions: Toward what ends ought theological education to strive? What are the means appropriate to the achievement of these ends? By approaching these questions from the basic moral and religious imperatives of the Christian faith, we may find solutions that are more consistent with the basic tenets of Christianity and with fundamental human values than were those provided by either Protestant or Catholic theologies of the past.

These questions, however, must not be asked in the abstract, but in close conjunction with the new, emerging situation which is rapidly developing out of the confrontation of Christians and Jews in a democratic society. Such new perspectives and insights can be derived from a combination of two major sources: (1) a reexamination of the traditional theological formulations of both Christianity and Judaism, and (2) a concrete knowledge of the social, economic, political, and religious conditions of the Jews in America.

The development of new theological and sociological perspectives toward the Jews in America and in the world and the consequent improvement in Jewish-Christian relations represent a major challenge to Christians in this country. This challenge to renewal must be met by the concerted efforts of all members of the Christian community-- clergy and laity alike--but especially weighty is the burden of responsibility on the shoulders of Christian seminarians in America. As Professor Davies suggests in his paper: We now have given to us "a unique opportunity to open the gates of the Church to the Synagogue--

that is, to renew the dialogue that history has broken. The conditions are present for the Church and Synagogue to coexist in
mutual stimulus, respect and fruition. That the benefits to the
Church would be enormous we have no doubt; that the Synagogue
would also benefit we cannot but hope. . . . There can be few
more urgent tasks for the Church than to prepare for this
dialogue, that it might really be a <u>dialogue</u> and not a soliloquy,
that it might be marked by the radical frankness which alone
makes genuine dialogue possible."

This Conference did not penetrate completely the impasse
between the Church and the Synagogue, but it did point to the
existence of that impasse and opened several entrées to future
dialogue between Christian and Jewish seminarians. This is all
one can expect from a pioneering venture: that it cause a stir
and create a promise.

EIGHTEEN

Select bibliography

J. Bruce Long

I BIBLICAL STUDIES--OLD AND NEW TESTAMENTS

Baum, Gregory. The Jews and the Gospel: A Re-Examination of the New Testament. London: W. Newman & Co., Ltd., 1961. In reply to a book entitled Jésus et Israel by Jules Isaac, the author analyzes and correlates the attitude of Jesus toward his early followers and their attitudes toward him. Baum examines with careful erudition the relations between the people, the Synagogue, and the early Christian Church as reflected in the Gospels, the Acts of the Apostles, and the Epistles of St. Paul.

Bultmann, Rudolf. The Theology of the New Testament (2 vols., translated by Kendrick Grobel). New York: Charles Scribner's Sons, 1951 (Vol. 1), 1955 (Vol. II). The author, who is considered the most authoritative scholar of New Testament theology in this century, presents his subject by "setting forth the theological thoughts of the New Testament writings, both those that are explicitly developed (such as Paul's teaching on the Law) and those that are implicitly at work in narrative or exhortation, in polemic or consolation." With a firm rootage in the historical situation of the time, Bultmann brilliantly tells of the initial deposit of kerygma in the life and teachings of Jesus, and of the "theologies" of the Synoptic Gospels, Paul, and John which emerged from that kerygma.

Cadbury, Henry J. The Peril of Modernizing Jesus. New York: The Macmillan Company, 1937. A presentation of the author's thesis that Jesus was a Jew of the first century and not the twentieth.

Cullman, Oscar. The Christology of the New Testament (translated by Shirley C. Guthrie and Charles A. M. Hall). Philadelphia: Westminster Press, 1959. This study of the various names or titles that Jesus applied to himself and that others applied to him in the New Testament is concerned, not with the precise definition of his nature, as were the Church Fathers in the succeeding centuries, but with a comprehensive picture of Christ's person and work. After examining the significance of these titles in Judaism, the author proceeds to analyze the changes in coloring that occurred in Hellenism and the New Testament. He discusses such titles of Jesus as the Prophet, Suffering Servant, High Priest, Messiah, Son of Man, Lord, Savior, and Son of God.

Daube, David. The New Testament and Rabbinic Judaism. New York: John de Graff, Inc., 1956. A discussion of ancient and contemporary issues related to the Rabbinic background of the New Testament as indicated by direct quotations and literary allusions to the Rabbinic source material.

Davies, W. D. Christian Origins and Judaism. London: Darton, Longman & Todd, Ltd., 1962. Calling for the resumption of the quest of the historical Jesus "on a new level," by giving "deeper attention to the roots of Jesus in His own times," Davies pursues with scholarly rigor the "study of Christianity's origins within Judaism as an integral part of the Ancient-Roman-Greco-Oriental world." Among the topics covered are "Apocalyptic and Pharisaism," "The Dead Sea Scrolls and Christian Origins," "A Normative Pattern of Church Life in the New Testament," and "Paul and the Dead Sea Scrolls: Flesh and Spirit."

----- Paul and Rabbinic Judaism: Some Rabbinic Elements in
Pauline Theology. London: Society for Promoting Christian
Knowledge, 1948. This work is an attempt to set certain
pivotal aspects of Paul's life and thought against the background
of the contemporary Rabbinic Judaism, so as to reveal how,
despite his apostleship to the Gentiles, he remained as far as
possible a Hebrew to the Hebrews and baptized his Rabbinic
heritage into Christ. In his presentation of Paul as a Pharisee
who became a Christian, Davies includes the following headings: "Flesh and Sin," "First and Second Adam," "Paul as
Preacher to the Individual," "Christ the Wisdom of God,"
"The Old and New Obedience," "Old and New Hope,"
"Resurrection."

Davies, W. D., and D. Daube, editors. The Background of the
New Testament and Its Eschatology. London: Cambridge
University Press, 1956. This is an impressive array of
scholarly essays, compiled in honor of C. H. Dodd, dealing
with many of the major problems and issues of New Testa-
ment scholarship. Included in the collection are "Mythological
Background of the New Testament" (Riesenfeld), "Die ebion-
itische Wahrheit des Christentums" (Schoeps), "The Life of
Jesus: Some Tendencies in Present-day Research" (Manson),
"Acts and Eschatology" (Cadbury), "Le Caractère, à la fois
actuel et future, du salut dans la théologie paulinienne"
(Goguel), "Kerygma, Eschatology and Social Ethics" (Wilder).

Eichrodt, Walther. Theology of the Old Testament, Vol. 1 (translated by J. A. Baker). Philadelphia: Westminster Press, 1961.
The author states as his purpose, in the Preface to the English
Edition, "to present the religion of which the records are to
be found in the Old Testament as a self-contained entity ex-
hibiting, despite ever-changing historical conditions, a constant
basic tendency and character . . . to arrive at a new understanding of the religious world of the Old Testament precisely
in respect of its religious quality." Eichrodt's work can be
used profitably as a counterpart to Bultmann's Theology of the
New Testament.

Enslin, Morton Scott. Christian Beginnings. New York: Harper
& Row, Publishers (Torchbook), 1938. This detailed, well-
documented volume is written with a fine sense for both historical accuracy and dramatic liveliness. The Jewish background of the New Testament is delineated clearly and with
great sympathy. See also a companion volume, Literature

of the Christian Movement, a book-by-book exposition of the
New Testament literature, which has an excellent chapter on
apocalypticism.

Grant, Frederick C. An Introduction to New Testament Thought.
Nashville: Abingdon-Cokesbury Press, 1950. An analysis of
concepts under such headings as "God," "Christ," "Man."

Grant, Robert M. An Historical Introduction to the New Testament.
New York: Harper & Row, Publishers, 1963. This book will
make profitable reading only for the advanced student of the
New Testament. It deals with the New Testament as it reflects
the historical life of the early Church, and illuminates the
meaning of the New Testament books by describing the history
which stands behind them and the hours out of which they emerged.
Three approaches--literary, historical, theological--are combined into one.

The Interpreter's Dictionary of the Bible (4 vols.). Nashville:
Abingdon-Cokesbury Press, 1962. This set is a very useful
source of general information concerning the beliefs, practices, and institutions of Judaism and Christianity. Although
many of the articles once considered standared are being
rendered obsolete by subsequent research, the dictionary
is still the most all-inclusive compendium of information
concerning the two religions and such cults as those of Mithras,
Osiris, and Isis.

Isaac, Jules. Jésus et Israel. Paris: A. Michel, 1948. In what is
more a personal inspection and evaluation of the life of Jesus as
recorded in the Gospels than a technical scholarly exegisis of
Scripture, the author, showing great sympathy for the person
of Jesus, "maintains that in the conflict between Judaism and
Christianity the preachers and teachers of the Church have
created a doctrine of contempt of the Jewish people and in-
spired a secular legislation of social debasement of the Jews.
Christian teaching has reinforced and justified the antisemitism
of pagan antiquity [Gregory Baum, The Jews and the Gospel,
p. 2.]."

Klausner, Joseph. From Jesus to Paul (translated from the Hebrew
by William F. Stinespring). Boston: Beacon Press, 1961. Interpreting the origins and early development of Christianity within
the context of the pagan and Jewish thought of the period, this
work gives the reader an understanding of the common heritage
of Judaism and Christianity, and the issues which divide them.

----- Jesus of Nazareth: His Life, Times, and Teaching (translated from the Hebrew by Herbert Danby). New York: The

Macmillan Company, 1953. A presentation of the life of
Jesus in context of the historical, religious, and socio-
economic background of his time.

----- The Messianic Idea in Israel from Its Beginning to the
Completion of the Mishnah (translated from the Hebrew by
W. F. Stinespring). New York: The Macmillan Company,
1955. An historical survey of the Messianic idea in the period
of the Prophets, the books of the Apocrypha and Pseudepigrapha,
and the period of the Tannaim.

Neher, André. Moses and the Vocation of the Jewish People (translated by Irene Marinoff). Men of Wisdom Series No. 7. New
York: Harper & Row, Publishers (Torchbook), 1959. The
author discusses the historical Moses, his calling and vocation,
and the origins and development of the Jewish religion.

Parkes, James. The Foundations of Judaism and Christianity.
Chicago: Quadrangle Books, 1960. The author, a Christian
scholar with great sympathy for a mutual understanding
between Jews and Christians, presents here the fruits of an
earnest and insightful search for the common foundations of
the two religious traditions.

Sandmel, Samuel. The Genius of Paul: A Study of History. New
York: Farrar, Straus, & Cudahy, 1958. A presentation of the
salient features of Paul's theology in light of his Jewish background.

----- A Jewish Understanding of the New Testament. Alumni
Publications Series. New York: Hebrew Union College Press,
1956. A semitechnical study of the literature of the New
Testament, beginning with an analysis of the historical circumstances and background of the era and concluding with a
section devoted to the significance of the New Testament.

Schoeps, H. J. Paul: The Theology of the Apostle in the Light
of Jewish Religious History (translated by Harold Knight).
Philadelphia: Westminster Press, 1961. This competent
scholarly study of Pauline theology is written by a Jew "who
wishes to do justice to the Judaism whence Paul sprang." In
his presentation the author includes the following headings:
"Eschatology of the Apostle Paul," "Paul's Teaching about
the Laws," "Perspectives of the History of Religions in
Paulinism."

Winter, Paul. On the Trial of Jesus. Berlin: Walter D. E. Gruyter
& Co., 1961. A critical evaluation by a European Jewish scholar
of certain aspects of the Gospel accounts of the arrest, trial,
and crucifixion of Jesus.

Zeitlin, Solomon. Who Crucified Jesus? (fourth edition). New
York: Bloch Publishing Company, 1964. This is an historical
study of the background and development of the first-century
Church, as that history was centered around the trial and
crucifixion of Jesus. The major thesis of the book is that
neither the modern Jew nor his ancestors were responsible in
any way whatsoever for the death of Jesus.

II HISTORY--JEWISH AND CHRISTIAN

Baeck, Leo. The Essence of Judaism (rendition by Irving Howe
based on the translation by Victor Grubenwieser and Leonard
Pearl). New York: Schocken Books, 1961. Originally published
in 1905, this work remains one of the widely acclaimed studies
of the nature of the underlying ideas of Judaism and their historical development.
----- This People Israel: The Meaning of Jewish Existence
(translated by Albert H. Friedlander). New York: Holt,
Rinehart and Winston, 1965. Begun in a German concentration
camp and completed in the United States when the author was
in his seventies, this book contains a survey both of Jewish
history and of the content of Judaism. It is "not a history but
a philosophy of history . . . a historiosophy--a religious interpretation of Jewish existence in the spirit of the great Biblical
historians, and authors of Kings and Chronicles, who saw in
the human events they were describing the guiding hand of God,
the arbiter of history."
Daniélou, Jean, and Henri Marrou. The Christian Centuries: A
New History of the Catholic Church. Vol. I: The First Six
Hundred Years (translated by Vincent Cronin). New York:
McGraw-Hill Book Company, 1964. Written in clear readable
prose, this work will benefit both scholar and informed general reader. "Catholic and Protestant students of each Church
history can only unite in gratitude to its authors for what is
now, and undoubtedly will remain for a long time, the only
comprehensive modern study of the subject. It is clear, in-
cisive, even brilliant. It is, in the most inclusive sense of
the word, catholic [review by R. M. Grant, Journal of Religion, July 1965]."
Davis, Moshe. The Emergence of Conservative Judaism: The
Historical School in Nineteenth Century America. Philadelphia:
The Jewish Publication Society of America, 1963. The author

presents a moving and knowledgeable account of the "emergence
of Conservative Judaism" in America--developing out of several
waves of migration to America, adjustment to a new sociopoliti-
cal situation, the discovery of individual liberty and opportunity,
and the search for personal and group identity. Davis also discusses the struggle for an education system, the development
of a Jewish periodical press, and the evolving communal order.

Flannery, E. H. The Anguish of the Jews: Twenty-three Centuries
of Anti-Semitism. New York: The Macmillan Company, 1965.
Comments from the dust jacket: "This book, the first written
by a Catholic priest on the history of anti-Semitism, begins
with the Greek and Egyptian attitudes that formed the base root
for much of what followed during the Christian era. It traces
the development of anti-Semitism through the periods of the
early Church, the fall of Rome, the Dark Ages, the Renais-
sance, and into modern times. The author's method is a
century-by-century development. . . . The result is a pains-
taking account of the guilt that casts its shadow over many,
if not all, of Western Civilization's proudest accomplishments."

Hay, Malcolm. Foot of Pride: The Pressure of Christendom on
the People of Israel for 1900 Years. Boston: Beacon Press,
1950. A Scottish Catholic presents a provocative and thorough
history of the doctrine of anti-Semitism and discusses various
atrocities against the Jews from the time of John Chrysostom
in the fourth century to the collapse of the Hitler regime and
the establishment of the State of Israel.

Parkes, James. Anti-Semitism: A Concise World-History. Chicago:
Quadrangle Books, 1962. The author discusses such topics as
group prejudice, psychology of religion, the Christian roots of
anti-Semitism, the anti-Semitic onslaught in the modern world,
and "the sterilization of prejudice."

----- The Conflict of the Church and the Synagogue. Philadelphia:
The Jewish Publication Society of America, 1961. This classic
study of the origins and causes of the Jewish Ghetto in medieval
Europe begins with an account of the Jews in the Roman world
and traces Jewish relations with pagans and Christians through
the early Middle Ages.

Schwartzman, S. D. Reform Judaism in the Making. New York:
Union of American Hebrew Congregations, 1955. In an historical account of the rise and development of Reform Judaism
in Europe and its transition to America, the author includes
examinations of its organization, principles, and practices.
The work is written to inform both the specialist in Jewish history
and the interested general reader.

III JUDAISM AND CHRISTIANITY

Baeck, Leo. Judaism and Christianity (translated by Walter
  Kaufmann). Philadelphia: The Jewish Publication Society of
  America, 1961. Five scholarly essays deal with the variety
  of attitudes and institutions of the two religions. Included
  in the presentations are "The Faith of Paul" and "The Gospel
  as a Document of the History of the Jewish Faith."
The Bridge: A Yearbook of Judaeo-Christian Studies. Edited by
  John M. Oesterreicher. New York: Pantheon Books, 1955
  (Vol. I), 1956 (Vol. II), 1958 (Vol. III), 1962 (Vol. IV). As
  the title indicates, this is a yearbook of Jewish-Christian
  studies, conducted by the Institute for Judaeo-Christian Studies,
  Seton Hall University. The stated purpose is to "show the Unity
  of God's design as it leads from the Law to the Gospel," to
  quicken the memory of Christians to their religious past, and
  to foster a creative dialogue between Christians and Jews.
  Each volume contains studies, perspectives, surveys, and
  book reviews.
Buber, Martin. Two Types of Faith: The Interpenetration of
  Judaism and Christianity (translated by Norman P. Goldhawk).
  New York: Harper & Row, Publishers (Torchbook), 1961. A
  theological inquiry into Pharisaic Judaism and early Christianity, analyzing differences and similarities of the two types
  of faith.
Glock, Charles Y., and Rodney Stark. Christian Beliefs and Anti-
  Semitism. New York: Harper & Row, Publishers, 1966. This
  study assumes that Christianity and anti-Semitism are historically linked and proceeds to inquire as to whether the link
  remains unbroken today or, as some observers have suggested,
  whether the Church now functions as a vehicle to transcend
  anti-Semitic attitudes. The findings of an extensive sociological
  survey of the "religious roots of anti-Semitism" support the
  contention that religious particularism leads naturally to anti-
  Semitism.
Gordis, Robert. The Root and the Branch: Judaism and the Free
  Society. Chicago: University of Chicago Press, 1962. An enlightening study of the insights of the Jewish tradition into the
  matters of intergroup relations, Church and State, education,
  politics, and international affairs.
Herberg, Will. Protestant-Catholic-Jew: An Essay in American
  Religious Sociology. Garden City: Doubleday and Company
  (Anchor Book), 1960. A sociological study of the interrela-

tionship of the three major religious groups in America,
with an examination of the religious and sociological significance of the most recent religious revivals.

Heschel, Abraham. Between God and Man: An Interpretation of
Judaism. New York: Harper & Row, Publishers, 1959. A
compilation of Professor Heschel's essays, providing a bird's-
eye view of the essence of Judaism and the Jewish tradition.

Isaac, Jules. The Teaching of Contempt: Christian Roots of Anti-
Semitism (translated by H. Weaver). New York: Holt, Rinehart
and Winston, 1964. The author presents a most arresting view
of the Christian sources and causes of anti-Semitism as "the
deepest ones of all." The book includes a summary statement
of Isaac's earlier volume Jésus et Israel.

Israel en de kerk. The Hague: Lectuurbureau der Nederlands
Hervormde Kerk, 1959. An officially commissioned study
dealing with the relation between the Church and Israel, this
essay repeats what the former has often said, namely, that
Christianity is indebted to the legacy of Judaism. But it goes
further. It pioneers with the assumption that Israel and the
Church stand in mutual need of each other in that the message
of each depends upon the witness of the other. The English
translation of this essay, produced by special commission
under appointment of the General Synod of the Reformed
Church of the Netherlands, is forthcoming.

Sandmel, Samuel. We Jews and Jesus. New York: Oxford University Press, 1965. This is a scholarly but readable account
of the history of Jewish-Christian relations, discussed under
five headings: "Early Christianity and Jewish Background,"
"The Divine Christ," "Jesus the Man," "The Jewish Reader
and the Gospels," and "Towards a Jewish Attitude to Christianity." The author gives a résumé of premodern Jewish approaches to Jesus; the approach of the modern Jew presented
in the light of scholarship, both Christian and Jewish, during
the past century and a half; and the implications of this approach to Christian-Jewish relations in modern times.

Sartre, Jean-Paul. Anti-Semite and Jew. New York: Schocken Books,
1948. In a disturbing and thought-provoking series of essays
the French existentialist philosopher addresses himself to the
problem of anti-Semitism with the kind of fearless moral vindictive against it for which he is well-known.

Schoeps, H. J. The Jewish-Christian Argument: A History of
Modern Dialogue (third edition, translated by David E. Green).
New York: Holt, Rinehart and Winston, 1963. This compre-

hensive and exciting history of the theological controversies between Judaism and Christianity ranges from those of the early Church Fathers and the Rabbis of the Talmudic period to the present debate between Karl Schmidt and Martin Buber.

IV ECUMENISM; VATICAN COUNCIL II

Brown, Robert McAfee. Observer in Rome: A Protestant Report on the Vatican Council. Garden City: Doubleday and Company, 1964. A Protestant observer at the Vatican Council gives a week-by-week account of the various "goings-on," covering almost every facet of the life and work of the Council: theological, ecclesiological, political, and "social."

Congar, Yves. Report from Rome on the First Session of the Vatican Council. The Christian Living Series. London: Geoffrey Chapman, 1963. The first session of Vatican II is recorded and interpreted by one of the Catholic Church's leading contemporary theologians. From the dust jacket comes the comment: "His brilliant theological mind makes as clear as daylight what issues were really involved, what developments really took place, how these are relevant to the living Church."

Häring, Bernhard. The Johannine Council: Witness to Unity (translated from the German by Edwin G. Kaiser). New York: Herder & Herder, 1963. This "theological appraisal" of Vatican II by one of the delegates includes the following topics: "Divine Revelation and the Mystery of Unity," "Moral Message of the Church," "Liturgy and the Mystery of Faith," "College of Bishops and the Roman Curia," "Social Message of the Church," "Need for Renewal in the Church." Of particular interest to all readers is the inclusion of the address of John XXIII at the opening of the Council.

Journal of Ecumenical Studies. Vol. I, No. 1, 1964. The stated purpose of this journal, published by Duquesne University Press, is "to provide the English-speaking world with a periodical devoted to serious . . . examination of the issues which concern Catholic, Protestant and orthodox Christians . . . renounces polemic. It intends to be a medium for candid analysis of the multitude of issues which provide opportunities for common faith and action in the future, as they have been occasions of dispute and schism in the past." Articles in the first issue were contributed by men active in the ecumenical effort: Cullmann, Frölich, Barth, Baum, Brown, Küng, and Tavard.

Küng, Hans, and others, editors. Council Speeches of Vatican II. New York: Sheed & Ward, 1964. This collection of major theological and ecclesiological statements made during the first session of Vatican II is presented under four major headings: "Self-awareness of the Church," "Renewal of the Church," "Reunion of All Christians," and "Dialogue with the World." These speeches, in the words of the editors, "solidify the gains, challenge the contemporary Church to action, and tell of what lies ahead."

Novak, Michael. The Open Church: Vatican II, Act II. New York: The Macmillan Company, 1964. This meticulous but dramatically written chronicle of the events of Vatican II, first and second sessions, intersperses among the day-to-day accounts of the major events liberal quotations from the speeches and daily communiques, to which the author had firsthand access. It concludes with an eye-opening statement, the purpose of which is to "chart the path for the development of the Open Church of the future."

Swidler, Leonard J., editor. Scripture and Ecumenism: Protestant, Catholic, Orthodox, and Jewish. Duquesne University Studies, Theological Series. Pittsburgh: Duquesne University Press, 1965. Nine papers delivered at the annual ecumenical seminar held at Duquesne University in the spring of 1964 are combined here in a volume having one of the broadest scopes of any recent literature on ecumenism. It includes responses from the Jewish community and from the three sectors of the Christian community to provide a dimension lacking in most books of this type. Subjects considered include tradition, the Bible, and Christian unity.

Wolf, Donald, and James Schall, editors. Current Trends in Theology. Garden City: Doubleday and Company, 1965. This is a kind of "state of the union" message, presenting a comprehensive examination and evaluation of all phases of the life and thought of the Catholic Church today. Among the topics discussed are "A Brief History of Catholic Theology," "Modern Trends in Theological Method," "Rediscovery of the Bible," "Contemporary Liturgical Revival," "Authority in the Church," and "American-Catholic Theories of Church-State Relations." Written with both Catholic and non-Catholic readers in mind, the stated purpose of the book is to "make clear to both groups the relevance of Catholicism to the many problems of our age."